VOGUE KNITTING

PILLOWS

VOGUE KNITTING

PILLOWS

THE BUTTERICK® PUBLISHING COMPANY
NEW YORK

THE BUTTERICK® PUBLISHING COMPANY
161 Avenue of the Americas
New York, New York 10013

THE BUTTERICK® PUBLISHING COMPANY and colophon
are registered trademarks of Butterick® Company, Inc.

Manufactured in the United States of America

1 3 5 7 9 10 8 6 4 2

Library of Congress Card Catalog Number: 97-077511

ISBN 1-57389-007-3

First Edition

TABLE OF CONTENTS

INTRODUCTION

In a world where everyone is constantly in a rush and on the move, finding "time-out" for yourself can be next to impossible. "I wish I had more time to knit" is the universal cry of all who love the craft. The truth is you do have time! A commute by bus or train, an endless wait in the doctor's office—even a class lecture—all provide the perfect opportunity to pull out your needles. The projects in the *Knitting on the Go* series are designed for just such spare moments. Compact pieces—small in scale, but big in creative outlet—that you can take along with you.

Pillows are the perfect portable project, requiring minimal investment in time and materials. Don't be afraid to challenge your skills—the exciting array of designs featured in this book provides great opportunities to try out new stitch patterns and techniques.

Get creative—the rules loosen up when it comes to pillows. The selection of beautiful yarns used in the designs photographed should be viewed as a starting point—feel free to substitute your own choices. Pillows are wonderful for using up leftover odds and ends or for splurging on a one-of-a-kind yarn. Feel free to experiment with color and texture—just be sure to make a test swatch for gauge. When you're happy with the results, you're ready to knit!

So pick a pattern, grab your needles and get ready to **KNIT ON THE GO!**

THE BASICS

Pillows, or "cushions" as they're called in some countries, are perfect for experimenting with yarn and color and for developing skills by trying out new techniques. We've taken care to set out some basics, so you can seize the opportunity to challenge yourself and produce beautifully knitted pillows for your home or for giving as gifts.

YARN SELECTION

For an exact reproduction of the piece photographed, use the yarn listed in the materials section of the pattern. We've selected yarns that are readily available in the U.S. and Canada at the time of printing. The Resources list on page 94 provides addresses of yarn distributors. Contact them for the name of a retailer in your area.

YARN SUBSTITUTION

You may wish to substitute yarns. Perhaps a spectacular yarn matches the decor of your home, maybe you view small-scale projects as a chance to incorporate leftovers from your yarn stash, or the yarn specified may not be available in your area. Pillow projects allow you to be as creative as you like, but you'll need to knit to the given gauge to obtain the knitted measurements with the substitute yarn (see "Gauge" on page 11). Make pattern adjustments (such as adding more rows to make the pillow a square) where necessary, or change the size of the pillow form if your gauge alters the dimensions. Be sure to consider how different yarn types (chenille, mohair, bouclé, etc.) will affect the final appearance of the pillow and the ease of care.

To facilitate yarn substitution, *Vogue Knitting* grades yarn by the standard stitch gauge obtained in Stockinette stitch. You'll find a grading number in the "Materials" section of the pattern, immediately following the fiber type of the yarn. Look for a substitute yarn that falls into the same

---

YARN SYMBOLS

① Fine Weight
(29-32 stitches per 4"/10cm)
Includes baby and fingering yarns, and some of the heavier crochet cottons. The range of needle sizes is 0-4 (2-3.5mm).

② Lightweight
(25-28 stitches per 4"/10cm)
Includes sport yarn, sock yarn, UK 4-ply and lightweight DK yarns. The range of needle sizes is 3-6 (3.25-4mm).

③ Medium Weight
(21-24 stitches per 4"/10cm)
Includes DK and worsted, the most commonly used knitting yarns. The range of needle sizes is 6-9 (4-5.5mm).

④ Medium-heavy Weight
(17-20 stitches per 4"/10cm)
Also called heavy worsted or Aran. The range of needle sizes is 8-10 (5-6mm).

⑤ Bulky Weight
(13-16 stitches per 4"/10cm)
Also called chunky. Includes heavier Icelandic yarns. The range of needle sizes is 10-11 (6-8mm).

⑥ Extra-bulky Weight
(9-12 stitches per 4"/10cm)
The heaviest yarns available. The range of needle sizes is 11 and up (8mm and up).

GAUGE

Most pillow patterns don't rely on a perfect fit as a knitted garment would, but it is still important to knit a gauge swatch. Without correct gauge a colorwork pattern may become distorted and patterns with shaped pieces (such as the Pompom Pyramids) may take on different proportions.

Patterns usually state gauge over a 4"/10cm span, however, it's beneficial to make a larger test swatch. This gives a more precise stitch gauge, a better idea of the appearance and drape of the knitted fabric, and gives you a chance to familiarize yourself with the stitch pattern. Knit your swatch in Stockinette stitch, unless otherwise specified, and make separate swatches for each pattern stitch when indicated.

The type of needles used—straight, circular, wood or metal—will influence gauge, so knit your swatch with the needles you plan to use for the project. Measure gauge as illustrated below. Try different needle sizes until your sample measures the required number of stitches and rows. *To get fewer stitches to the inch/cm, use a larger needle; to get more stitches to the inch/cm, use a smaller needle.* It's a good idea to keep your gauge swatch in order to test blocking and cleaning methods.

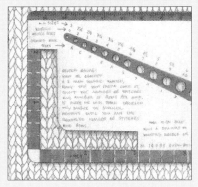

category. The suggested needle size and gauge on the ball band should be comparable to that on the Yarn Symbols chart on page 10.

After you've successfully gauge-swatched a substitute yarn, you'll need to figure out how much of the substitute yarn the project requires. First, find the total length of the original yarn in the pattern (multiply number of balls by yards/meters per ball). Divide this figure by the new yards/meters per ball (listed on the ball band). Round up to the next whole number. The answer is the number of balls required.

FOLLOWING CHARTS

Charts provide a convenient way to follow colorwork, lace, cable and other stitch patterns at a glance. *Vogue Knitting* stitch charts utilize the universal knitting language of "symbolcraft." Unless otherwise indicated, read charts from right to left on right side (RS) rows and from left to right on wrong side (WS) rows, repeating any stitch and row repeats as directed in the pattern. Posting a self-adhesive note under your working row is an easy way to keep track of your place on a chart.

Two main types of colorwork are explored in this book.

Intarsia

Intarsia is accomplished with separate bobbins of individual colors. This method is ideal for large blocks of color or for motifs that aren't repeated close together. When changing colors, always pick up the new color and wrap around the old color to prevent holes.

Stranding

When motifs are closely placed, colorwork is accomplished by stranding along two or more colors per row, creating "floats" on the wrong side of the fabric. When using this method, twist yarns on WS to prevent holes and strand loosely to keep knitting from puckering.

Note that yarn amounts have been calculated for the colorwork method suggested in the pattern. Knitting a stranded pattern with intarsia bobbins will take less yarn, while stranding an intarsia pattern will require more yarn.

LACE

Lace has long been a favorite accent for the home, and this book includes several lace pillows. Knitted lace is formed with "yarn overs," which create an eyelet hole, in combination with decreases that create directional effects. To make a yarn over (yo), pass the yarn over the right-hand needle to form a new loop. On most RS rows of lace knitting there is one decrease to match each yarn over so that the stitch count remains even. On WS rows the yarn overs are usually treated as a stitch. In some cases, a double yo (or yo twice) is worked, then treated as two stitches on the following row. If you're new to lace knitting, it's a good idea to count the stitches at the end of each WS row. Making a gauge swatch in the stitch pattern enables you to practice a new lace pattern. Instead of binding off the swatch, place the final row on a holder, as the bind-off tends to pull in the stitches and distort the gauge.

BLOCKING

Blocking is the best way to shape pattern pieces and smooth knitted edges in preparation for sewing together. However, some yarns, such as chenilles and ribbons, do not benefit from blocking. Choose a blocking method according to the yarn care label and, when in doubt, test-block on your gauge swatch.

Wet Block Method

Using rust-proof pins, pin pieces to measurements on a flat surface and lightly dampen using a spray bottle. Allow to dry before removing pins.

Steam Block Method

Pin pieces to measurements with WS of

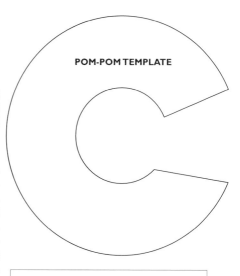

knitting facing up. Steam lightly, holding the iron 2"/5cm above the knitting. Do not press the iron onto the pieces, as it will flatten the stitches.

TRIMS

Knitted pillows may be decorated with a wide variety of embellishments. Consider the interesting use of purchased trims—tassels, pom-pom tapes and buttons—as well as handmade trims. Two favorites created with yarn—pom-poms and tassels—are illustrated at right and below. In order to make these trims plump and appealing, be generous with the yarn (trims have been figured into our yarn amounts).

FULLING

Two of our pillow patterns make use of "fulling," a washing process for woolen knits (sometimes referred to as felting)

POM-POM

1 *Following the template, cut two circular pieces of cardboard.*

2 *Hold the two circles together and wrap the yarn tightly around the cardboard several times. Secure and carefully cut the yarn.*

3 *Tie a piece a yarn tightly between the two circles. Remove the cardboard and trim the pom-pom to the desired size.*

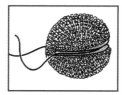

TASSELS

Cut a piece of cardboard to the desired length of the tassel. Wrap yarn around the cardboard. Knot a piece of yarn tightly around one end, cut as shown, and remove the cardboard. Wrap and tie yarn around the tassel about 1"/2.5cm down from the top to secure the fringe.

that creates a more dense and fuzzy fabric. Water, soap, extreme temperature change and friction cause wool fibers to entangle, condensing the knitted fabric. Fulling can easily be accomplished in the washing machine and is described in the individual patterns. As results differ with particular machines, you may wish to practice fulling on a swatch. Make any adjustments to pillow backs and pillow forms after fulling.

CARE

Remove the pillow form or fiberfill and clean your pillow as necessary. Refer to the yarn label for the recommended cleaning method. Most of the wool or cotton pillows in the book can be washed by hand (or in the machine on a gentle or wool cycle) in lukewarm water with a mild detergent. Do not agitate, and don't soak for more than 10 minutes. Rinse gently with tepid water, then fold in a towel and gently press the water out. Lay flat to dry, away from excessive heat and light.

PILLOW FORMS

The imaginative pillows in this book are knit in a variety of shapes and sizes. Knitted measurements are given along with a suggested size for pillow forms, where available. Keep in mind that size may alter when using substitute yarns.

Most commercial pillow forms are stuffed with non-allergenic polyester fiberfill or foam. Other popular fillers are down and feathers, woolen fleece, cotton batting and buckwheat hulls. If the required finished size is not commercially available, you can purchase loose fiberfill and simply stuff the pillow or make your own pillow insert with the fabric of your choice.

SELECTING FABRIC

Several pillow patterns call for fabric backing, or, as with the Silk Lavender Sachets and Lace Overlay, fabric pillow covers. The materials section lists the type of fabric and yardage required. Pillow backs provide the perfect opportunity to use leftovers or to splurge on a small quantity of luxury fabric. One consideration for fabric selection is care— pair a fabric with a yarn of a similar care requirement. If the pillow will be placed in a high-traffic area, choose durable and easy-care fabric. Before cutting fabric, prewash and press following the manufacturer's care label. When cutting the pillow back, place the grain of the fabric in the same direction as the grain of the knitting (lengthwise). Fabric pillow covers may be sewn by hand or machine. Knitted pillows with fabric backs are best sewn by hand using a slipstitch and matching sewing thread.

KNITTING TERMS AND ABBREVIATIONS

approx approximately

beg begin(ning)

bind off Used to finish an edge and keep stitches from unraveling. Lift the first stitch over the second, the second over the third, etc. (UK: cast off)

cast on A foundation row of stitches placed on the needle in order to begin knitting.

CC contrast color

cm centimeter(s)

cont continu(e)(ing)

dec decrease(ing)—Reduce the stitches in a row (knit 2 together).

dpn double pointed needle(s)

foll follow(s)(ing)

g gram(s)

garter stitch Knit every row. Circular knitting: knit one round, then purl one round.

inc increase(ing)—Add stitches in a row (knit into the front and back of a stitch).

k knit

k2tog knit 2 stitches together

LH left-hand

m meter(s)

MI make one stitch—With the needle tip, lift the strand between last stitch worked and next stitch on the left-hand needle and knit into the back of it. One stitch has been added.

MC main color

mm millimeter(s)

oz ounce(s)

p purl

p2tog purl 2 stitches together

pat pattern

pick up and knit (purl) Knit (or purl) into the loops along an edge.

pm place markers—Place or attach a loop of contrast yarn or purchased stitch marker as indicated.

rem remain(s)(ing)

rep repeat

rev St st reverse Stockinette stitch—Purl right-side rows, knit wrong-side rows. Circular knitting: purl all rounds. (UK: reverse stocking stitch)

rnd(s) round(s)

RH right-hand

RS right side(s)

sc single crochet (UK: double crochet)

sl slip—An unworked stitch made by passing a stitch from the left-hand to the right-hand needle as if to purl.

st(s) stitch(es)

St st Stockinette stitch—Knit right-side rows, purl wrong-side rows. Circular knitting: knit all rounds. (UK: stocking stitch)

tbl through back of loop

tog together

WS wrong side(s)

wyif with yarn in front

wyib with yarn in back

work even Continue in pattern without increasing or decreasing. (UK: work straight)

yd yard(s)

yo yarn over—Make a new stitch by wrapping the yarn over the right-hand needle. (UK: yfwd, yon, yrn)

BERBER PILLOWS

A harmonious blend of vivid colors

Linen-stitch Berber pillows designed by Jean Shafer Albers resemble rustic, woven rugs. Several colors are held together in unique combinations while fabric backings make for easy construction.

KNITTED MEASUREMENTS
16" x 16"/40.5cm x 40.5cm

MATERIALS

For all versions (makes 3 pillows)

■ 2 4oz/113g skeins (each approx 190yd/173m) of Brown Sheep *Lamb's Pride Worsted* (wool/mohair⑤) in #M-43 olive (A)

■ 1 skein #M-26 red (B)

■ 1 1¾oz/50g ball (approx 184yd/168m) of *Nature Spun Sports* (wool③) each in #N17 clay (C), #N13 brown (D), #N48 scarlet (E), #308 gold (F)

■ One pair size 7 (4.5mm) needles *or size to obtain gauge*

■ Bobbins

■ Fabric 17" x 17"/43cm x 43cm for each pillow back

■ Matching sewing thread

■ Sewing needle

■ Three pillow forms 16" x 16"/40.5cm x 40.5cm

GAUGE
20 sts and 40 rows to 4"/10cm over linen st, using size 7 (4.5mm) needles. *Take time to check gauge.*

Notes 1 Each version uses single strands of worsted weight and double strands of sport weight yarns.

2 When changing colors work first row of new color in St st, then cont in pat.

3 Use separate bobbins of yarn for each section of color.

4 Twist yarn on WS to prevent holes.

5 Colors for Colorway 2 are in ( ) and for Colorway 3 in [ ].

STITCHES USED

Linen Stitch (over an even number of sts)

Row 1 (RS) *P1, sl 1 purlwise wyib; rep from * to last 2 sts, p2.

Row 2 *K1, sl 1 purlwise wyif; rep from * to last 2 sts, k2.

Rep these 2 rows for linen st.

FRONT

With size 7 (4.5mm) needles and B (C&D) [C&F], cast on 80 sts and work in linen st, working color changes and rows as indicated on diagram (160 rows in total). Bind off firmly in pat.

FINISHING

Block piece. Press fabric ½"/1cm to WS on one side. With RS of Front and fabric tog, and matching folded edge to one side of pillow top, using small back st, sew 3 rem sides tog. Turn to RS and insert pillow form. Sew rem side closed.

Color key

- Olive (A)
- Red (B)
- Clay (C) & Brown (D)
- Clay (C) & Gold (F)
- Scarlet (E)

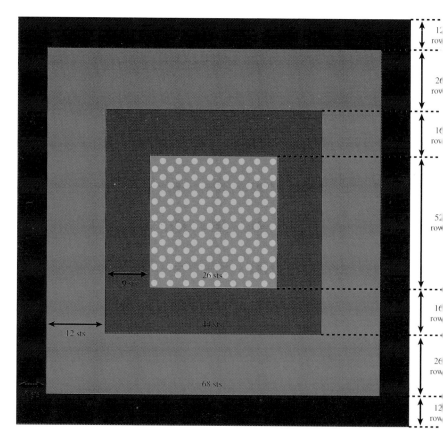

26 sts

9 sts

14 sts

12 sts

68 sts

12 rows

20 rows

10 rows

52 rows

10 rows

26 rows

12 rows

Nordic-inspired pillow with snowflake-motif flange designed by Shirley Paden. The two-color repeat pattern and snowflake border are knit in one piece, and the boldly-striped back has a center-buttoning closure.

KNITTED MEASUREMENTS

26" x 25"/66cm x 63.5cm with flange
(17" x 18¼"/44.5cm x 46.5cm actual pillow)

MATERIALS

■ 10 1¾oz/50g balls (each approx 116yd/106m) of Dale of Norway *Falk* (wool③) in #6842 aqua (MC)
■ 7 balls in #0017 white (CC)
■ One pair each sizes 4 and 5 (3.5 and 3.75mm) needles *or size to obtain gauge*
■ Tapestry needle
■ Stitch markers
■ Pillow form 18" x 18"/ 46cm x 46cm
■ 6 snaps

GAUGES

■ 24 sts and 30 rows to 4"/10cm over St st, using size 4 (3.5mm) needles.
■ 27 sts and 28.5 rows to 4"/10cm over chart 2, using size 5 (3.75mm) needles.
Take time to check gauges.
Note When changing colors, twist yarns on WS to prevent holes in work.

FRONT

With size 5 (3.75mm) needles and MC, cast on 179 sts. Work in St st for 2 rows.
Beg Chart 1: Row 1 (RS) Work 2 MC (selvage sts used for seam), work 25-st rep of chart 1 for 7 times, work 2 MC (selvage sts). Cont as established through chart row 25.

Next row (WS) 2 selvage sts, work row 26 of chart 1 over next 25 sts, place marker (pm), p1 MC, p123 MC, p1 MC, pm, work row 26 of chart 1 over next 25 sts, 2 selvage sts.

Next row (RS) 2 selvage sts, work row 27 of chart 1 over 25 sts, sl marker, k1 MC, work 6-st rep chart 2 for 20 times, then work first 3 sts of chart once more, k1 MC, sl marker, work row 27 of chart 1 over 25 sts, 2 selvage sts. Cont as established, working 1 MC st each side of chart 2, until there are 151 rows from beg. On next row, work MC only over center 125 sts, and cont 27 sts each side as established.

Next row (RS) Keeping first and last 2 sts in MC for selvage sts, work rem 175 sts in chart 1 for 25 rows. With MC, work in St st for 2 rows. Bind off purlwise with MC.

BACK (worked in 2 sections)

First Section

With size 4 (3.5mm) needles and MC, cast on 160 sts. Work in St st until piece measures 5"/12.5cm. Change to CC and cont in St st until piece measures 10"/25.5cm from beg. Change to MC and cont in St st until piece measures 14"/35.5cm from beg, then cont in k1, p1 rib for 1"/2.5cm, end with a WS row. Bind off in rib.

Second Section

Work as for first section from * to *, then cont in k1, p1 rib for 1"/2.5cm, end with a WS row. Bind off in rib.

FINISHING

Block pieces. With ribs overlapping each other, sew center side seam on back. With RS of back and front tog, sew all 4 seams, 2 sts in from sides and 2 rows in from cast-on and bound-off edges. Turn to RS. Using tapestry needle and MC, with wrong sides tog, backstitch front and back tog, around outside edges of chart 2, working in the center of the MC st at each side. Sew on snaps. Insert pillow form.

CHART 2

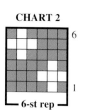

6

1

6-st rep

Color key

☐ White

▨ Aqua

CHART 1

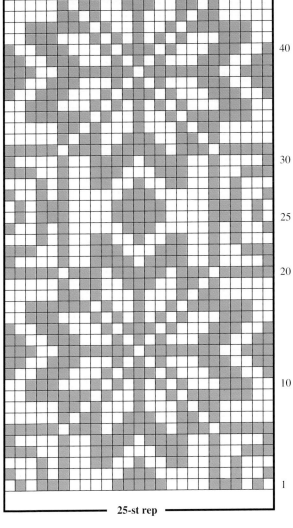

50

40

30

25

20

10

1

25-st rep

23

For Intermediate Knitters

Fall leaves take on new dimension in the hands of Nicky Epstein. In coordinating tweeds, they are trimmed with I-cord, crochet and duplicate stitch.

KNITTED MEASUREMENTS

Oak Leaf

14"/35.5cm at widest point, 22"/56cm at longest point, 3"/7.5cm thick

Maple Leaf

14"/35.5cm at widest point, 16"/40.5cm at longest point, 3"/7.5cm thick

Elm Leaf

14"/35.5cm at widest point, 16"/40.5cm at longest point, 3"/7.5cm thick

MATERIALS

Oak Leaf

■ 2 3½oz/100g skeins (each approx 183yd/167m) of Tahki *Donegal Tweed* (wool④) in #0803 green (MC)
■ 1 skein #0893 copper (CC)

Maple Leaf

■ 2 3½oz/100g skeins (each approx 183yd/167m) of Tahki *Donegal Tweed* (wool④) in #0893 copper (MC)
■ 1 skein #0824 teal (CC)

Elm Leaf

■ 2 3½oz/100g skeins (each approx 183yd/167m) of Tahki *Donegal Tweed* (wool④) in #0878 forest green (MC)
■ 1 skein #0880 brick (CC)
■ One pair size 7 (4.5mm) double-pointed needles (dpn)

All versions

■ One pair size 7 (4.5mm) needles *or size to obtain gauge*
■ Size G (4.5mm) crochet hook
■ Fiberfill
■ Stitch holder

GAUGE

16 sts and 22 rows to 4"/10cm over St st, using size 7 (4.5mm) needles. *Take time to check gauge.*

Oak Leaf

BACK

With size 7 (4.5mm) needles and MC, cast on 10 sts. Work foll chart rows 1-134 for back, shape as indicated. Bind off.

FRONT

With size 7 (4.5mm) needles and MC, cast on 10 sts. Work foll chart rows 1-24 for front, then cont with rows 25-134 as for back. Bind off.

FINISHING

Block pieces. With RS facing, crochet hook and CC, chain st veins to front and back foll chart.

Side Panel

With size 7 (4.5mm) needles and MC, cast on 14 sts. Work in St st for approx 78"/198cm, sl sts to holder. With WS tog, using crochet hook and CC, sc side panel to front. Adjust side panel, taking rows off or adding rows on for perfect fit, bind off, close side panel seam. Sc back to side panel, leaving opening for filling. Stuff with fiberfill and sc closed.

Maple Leaf

With size 7 (4.5mm) needles and MC, cast on 14 sts. Work chart rows 1-38. Work row 39 of chart as foll: K12, turn, sl rem 40 sts to a holder. Cont on these 12 sts only, work rows 40-50 for right tip, bind off. With RS facing, sl 40 sts from holder to needle, k to end of row.

Row 40 of Chart P12, turn, sl rem 28 sts to holder. Cont on 12 sts for left tip and work rows 41-51. Bind off. With WS facing, sl sts from holder to needle with 28 sts for center of leaf, and p to end of row. Cont to work rows 41-80 of chart, working 2nd set of tips same as first set, bind off.

FRONT
Work as for back.

FINISHING
Work finishing and Side Panel same as Oak Leaf. Work in St st for side panel for approx 62"/158cm.

Elm Leaf

Note Pillow is worked from top down.

BACK
With size 7 (4.5mm) needles and MC, cast on 3 sts. Work chart rows 1-82, shape as indicated. Work Row 83 of chart as foll: (RS) Bind off 2 sts, k until 21 sts are on RH needle, turn, sl rem 30 sts to holder. **Row 84 of Chart** Bind off 2 sts, p to end. Work to end of tip as indicated on chart. With RS facing, sl sts from holder to needle with 30 sts. Cont to work Row 83 of chart: K 7, bind off 2 sts, k to end. Work to end of 2nd tip as indicated on chart. With WS rejoin to rem 7 sts, work rows 84-98 as indicated on chart. Bind off.

FRONT
Work as for Back.

FINISHING
Block pieces.

I-cord
With CC and dpn, cast on 3 sts. *K3, do not turn. Slide sts to other end of needle and k3. Rep from * for I-cord. Make two cords approx 52"/132cm long and two cords approx 14"/35.5cm long. Sew shorter cords to Front and Back as center veins, using photo as inspiration.

Side Panel
With size 7 (4.5mm) needles and MC, cast on 14 sts. Work in St st for approx 50"/127cm, sl sts to holder. With WS tog, using crochet hook and MC, sc side panel to front. Adjust side panel, taking rows off or adding rows on for perfect fit, bind off, close side panel seam. Sc back to side panel, leaving opening for filling. Stuff with fiberfill and sc closed. With CC, sew longer cords around leaf edges.

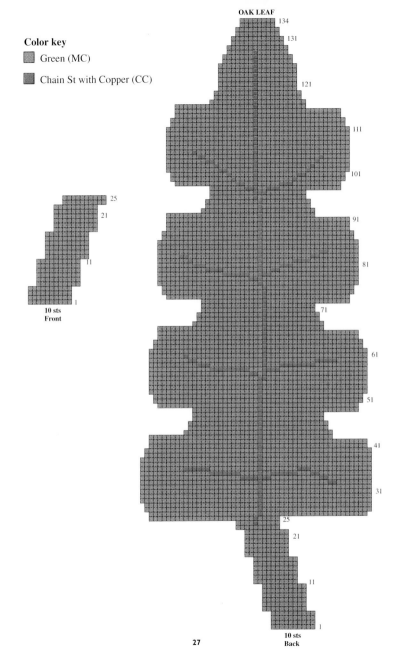

OAK LEAF

Color key
- Green (MC)
- Chain St with Copper (CC)

134
131
121
111
101
91
81
71
61
51
41
31
25
21
11
1

**10 sts
Back**

25
21
11
1

**10 sts
Front**

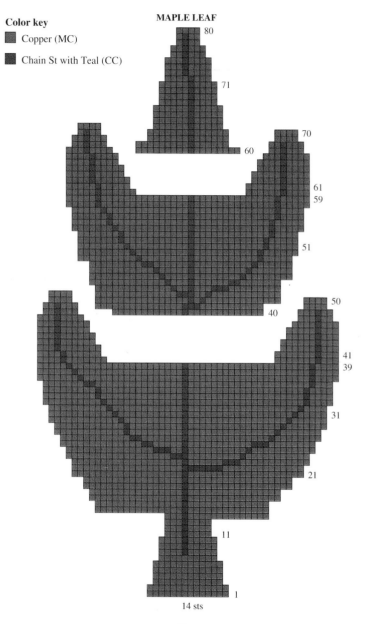

Color key
■ Copper (MC)
■ Chain St with Teal (CC)

MAPLE LEAF

80

71

70

60

61
59

51

50

40

41
39

31

21

11

1

14 sts

ELM LEAF

Color key

Forest Green (MC)

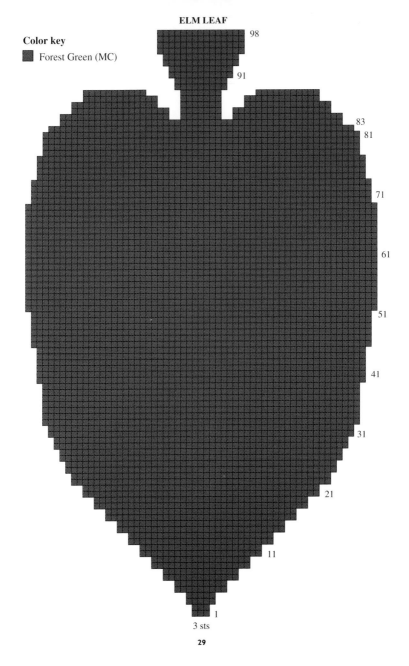

98

91

83

81

71

61

51

41

31

21

11

1

3 sts

Aran-influenced, tasseled pillows designed by Jean Moss. Panels of zigzag and interlocking diamonds are framed with seed-stitch columns. Tasseled corners and envelope closure make for a fine finish.

KNITTED MEASUREMENTS
18" x 18"/46cm x 46cm

MATERIALS

Gold Pillow

■ 12 .88oz/25g skeins (each approx 75yds/67m) of Rowan *Light Weight DK* (wool②) in #104 antique gold

Rose Pillow

■ 12 .88oz/25g skeins (each approx 75yds/67m) of Rowan *Light Weight DK* (wool②) in #411 dusty rose

Both versions

■ One pair each sizes 3 and 5 (3.25 and 3.75mm) needles *or size to obtain gauge*
■ Cable needle (cn)
■ Stitch markers
■ Tapestry needle
■ Pillow form 18" x 18"/46cm x 46cm

GAUGE
29 sts and 32 rows to 4"/10cm over chart pat, using larger needles. *Take time to check gauge.*

STITCH GLOSSARY

Seed st
Row 1 (RS) *K1, p1; rep from * to end.
Row 2 P the knit sts, and k the purl sts.
Rep row 2 for seed st.

2-st Right Twist (2RT)
On RS rows: K next 2 sts tog without removing sts from LH needle; k first st again, then sl both sts from LH needle.

On WS rows: P 2nd st on LH needle, without removing sts from LH needle; then p2tog (first st and st just worked), then sl both sts from LH needle.

2-st Left Twist (2LT)
With RH needle behind LH needle, k 2nd st on LH needle tbl; k first st through front loop, then sl both sts from LH needle.

2/1 Right Cable (2/1 RC)
Sl next st to cn and hold in *back*, k2, k1 from cn.

2/1 Left Cable (2/1 LC)
Sl next 2 sts to cn and hold in *front*, k1, k2 from cn.

GOLD PILLOW

BACK
With size 3 (3.25mm) needles, cast on 130 sts. Work in seed st for 1½"/4cm, end with a RS row. Change to larger needles.
Beg Charts: Next row (WS) Work 10 sts seed st as established, [14 sts chart 1, 10 sts chart 2 and beg with row 17]

twice, [14 sts chart 1, work 10 sts chart 2, beg with row 1] twice, 14 sts chart 1, 10 sts seed st. Cont as established, work 26-row rep of chart 1 and 32-row rep of chart 2 throughout. Work until piece measures 16½"/42cm from beg, end with a WS row. Change to smaller needles and work in seed st for 1½"/4cm, end with a WS row. Bind off in seed st.

FRONT

Work as for back until piece measures 18"/46cm.

Next 2 rows (hemline) Purl.

Flap Work in St st for 4"/10cm, end with a WS row. Bind off.

FINISHING

Block pieces to measurements. Fold flap to WS at hemline and sl st in place at sides. With tapestry needle and RS of front and back tog, backstitch 3 sides. Turn to RS.

TASSELS (Make 4)

Wind yarn 24 times around a 14"/35.5cm piece of cardboard. Thread longer strand yarn through loops at one end on cardboard and secure tightly, do not cut, cut loops at other end. Wrap yarn around tassel ¾"/2cm down from top, for ¾"/2cm, pass through center of tassel and use to secure tassel to pillow corner. Insert pillow form.

ROSE PILLOW

Work as for Gold Pillow.

Beg Chart: Next row (WS) Work 10 sts seed st as established, [14 sts chart 1, work 10 sts chart 2 and beg with row 1] twice, [14 sts chart 1, 10 sts chart 2 and beg with row 17] twice, 14 sts chart 1, 10 sts seed st. Complete as for Gold Pillow.

CHART 1

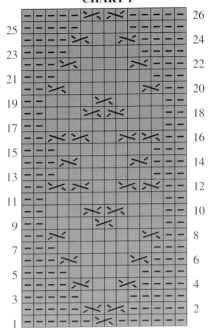

14 sts

Stitch key

- ▨ k on RS, p on WS
- ⊟ p on RS, k on WS
- ⟩⟨ 2 RT
- ⟨⟩ 2 LT
- ⟩╱ 2/1 RC
- ╲⟨ 2/1 LC

CHART 2

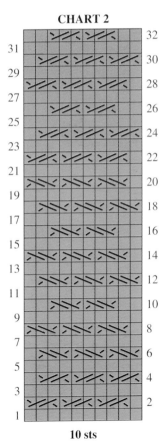

10 sts

For Intermediate Knitters

Cactus flower intarsia pillows created by Australian designer Jo Sharp. Swirling blossoms, accentuated by a twisted cord trim, are depicted in two exotic colorways.

KNITTED MEASUREMENTS
18½"/47 cm wide x 16"/40 cm long (without corded edging)

MATERIALS

Antique Beige Pillow
- 4 1¾oz/50g balls (each approx 107yd/98m) of Jo Sharp *Super Soft Extra Fine DK* (wool④) in #323 antique beige (MC)
- 1 ball each #318 forest green (A), #322 ginger (B), #325 mulberry (C), #319 violet (D), #324 lilac (E), #320 gold (F), #316 jade (G), #326 ruby (H), #327 navy (I), #332 terracotta (J)

Mulberry Pillow
- 4 1¾oz/50g balls (each approx 107yd/98m) of Jo Sharp *Super Soft Extra Fine DK* (wool④) in #325 mulberry (MC)
- 1 ball each #318 forest green (A), #323 antique beige (B), #322 ginger (C), #319 violet (D), #324 lilac (E), #320 gold (F), #316 jade (G), #326 ruby (H), #327 navy (I), #332 terracotta (J)

Both versions
- One pair size 6 (4mm) needles *or size to obtain gauge*
- Bobbins
- Tapestry needle
- Pillow form 18" x 18"/46cm x 46cm

GAUGE
20 sts and 30 rows to 4"/10cm over St st using size 6 (4mm) needles. *Take time to check gauge.*

Notes 1 Use separate bobbins of yarn for each section of color.
2 Twist yarn on WS to prevent holes.

FRONT
With size 6 (4mm) needles and MC, cast on 92 sts. Work 120 rows of chart. Bind off with MC.

BACK
With size 6 (4mm) needles and MC, cast on 92 sts. Work in St st for 120 rows. Bind off.

FINISHING
Block pieces. Sew three sides. Insert pillow form. Sew rem side, leaving small section at corner open for insertion of twisted cord ends.

TWISTED CORD
Cut 8 strands each 7yds/6.5m long of MC. Knot ends tog at both ends, ensuring lengths are even. Attach one end to a stable object. Twist other end clockwise until cord begins to curl. Placing both ends together, fold in half, knot firmly below first knots and allow cord to twist evenly. Cut off first 2 knots. Beg at opening, neatly sew cord along seams, looping and securing cord at each pillow corner (using photo as guide). Place ends into opening, and sew opening closed.

Color key

☐ Antique Beige (MC)

■ Forest Green (A)

■ Ginger (B)

■ Mulberry (C)

■ Violet (D)

☐ Lilac (E)

■ Gold (F)

☐ Jade (G)

■ Ruby (H)

■ Navy (I)

■ Terracotta (J)

ANTIQUE BEIGE PILLOW

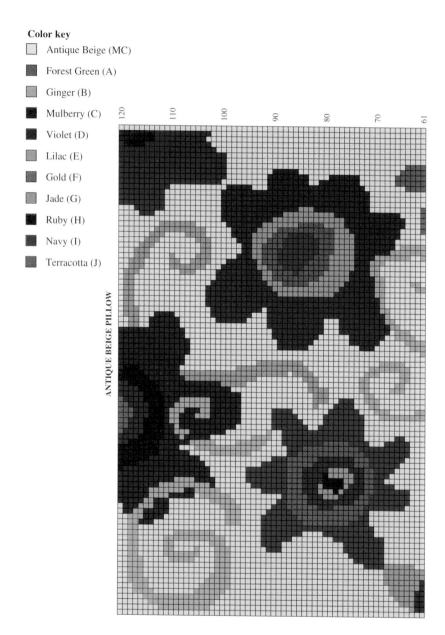

Color key

- ■ Mulberry (MC)
- ▨ Forest Green (A)
- ▦ Antique Beige (B)
- ▦ Ginger (C)
- ▨ Violet (D)
- ▦ Lilac (E)
- ▨ Gold (F)
- ▨ Jade (G)
- ■ Ruby (H)
- ▨ Navy (I)
- ▨ Terracotta (J)

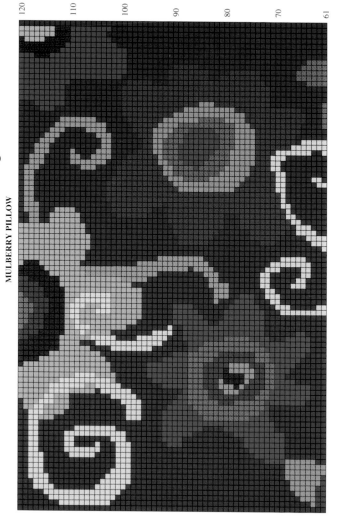

MULBERRY PILLOW

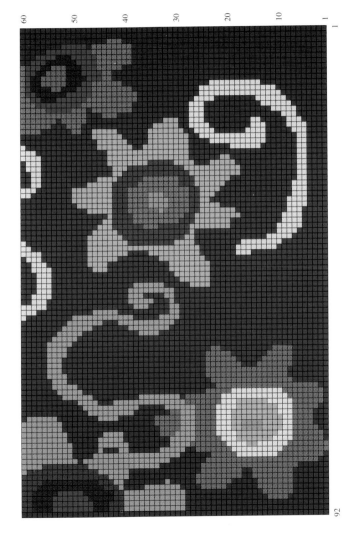

On a whimsical note...

For Intermediate Knitters

Pyramid pillows designed by Lila P. Chin use three shades of jewel-colored kettle-dyed yarn. Double seed stitch adds texture and pom-poms trim the corners.

KNITTED MEASUREMENTS

10"/27cm high x 12"/30cm wide

MATERIALS

Purple version

■ 1 3½oz/100g (each approx 137yd/127m) of Manos Del Uruguay *700 Tex* (wool⑤) in #62 medium purple (A), #50 lavender (B), #57 plum (C), #03 lilac (D)

Blue version

■ 1 3½oz/100g (each approx 137yd/127m) of Manos Del Uruguay *700 Tex* (wool⑤) in #43 teal (A), #04 light blue (B), #60 royal blue (C), #Q light teal (D)

Both versions

■ One pair of 7 (4.5mm) needles *or size to obtain gauge.*
■ Fiberfill
■ Tapestry needle

GAUGE

16 sts and 26 rows to 4"/10cm in double seed st using size 7 (4.5mm) *Take time to check gauge.*

STITCHES USED

Double Seed Stitch

Rows 1 and 2 *K1, p1; rep from * to end.
Rows 3 and 4 *P1, k1; rep from * to end.
Rep rows 1-4 for double seed st.

PANEL (make 4 panels, 1 each in A, B, C and D)

*With size 7 (4.5mm) needles and A, cast on 48 sts. Work in double seed st, dec 1 st at each side every 3rd row 22 times—4 sts. Bind off.

FINISHING

Sew 3 side panel pieces tog, leaving one side open. Stuff with fiberfill and sew rem side closed. Make one pom-pom in each color and attach to each point.

ENTRELAC PILLOW

Subtly-colored bouclé maximizes texture

Softly textured pillow designed by Bette Anne Lampers. Hand-painted yarn lends subtle, variegated coloring to the woven look of entrelac.

KNITTED MEASUREMENTS
20" x 20"/51cm x 51cm

MATERIALS
■ 5 3½oz/100g skeins (each approx 97yds/90m) of Colinette *Bracken* (wool⑤) in #75 moss
■ One pair size 7 (4.5mm) needles *or size to obtain gauge*
■ Approx 5yds/4.5m matching smooth yarn for finishing
■ Tapestry needle
■ Pillow form 20" x 20"/51cm x 51cm

GAUGE
14 sts and 26 rows to 4"/10cm over St st, using size 7 (4.5mm) needles (steam block swatch before measuring). *Take time to check gauge.*

Knitting-on cast on
1 Make a slip knot on LH needle. *Insert RH needle knitwise into stitch on LH needle. Wrap yarn around right needle as if to knit.
2 Draw yarn through st on needle to make new st, leaving previous st on LH needle.
3 Slip new stitch onto LH needle. Rep from * until required number of sts is cast on.

Make one (M1)
1 Insert LH needle from back to front into horizontal strand between last st worked and next st on LH needle.
2 Knit this strand through front loop to twist st.
Notes 1 Slip the sl sts purlwise. On RS rows sl st wyib, on WS rows wyif.
2 Sl sts loosely on pillow edges.

FRONT

Base Triangles (BT)
With size 7 (4.5mm) needles, cast on 2 sts.
Row 1 (RS) K2.
Row 2 Sl 1, p1, turn. Cast on 1 st (3 sts on LH needle).
Row 3 K3.
Row 4 Sl 1, p2, turn. Cast on 1 st (4 sts on LH needle).
Row 5 K4.
Row 6 Sl 1, p3, turn. Cast on 1 st.
Row 7 K5.
Row 8 Sl 1, p4, turn. Cast on 1 st.
Row 9 K6.
Row 10 Sl 1, p5, turn—One BT completed. Leaving first triangle on LH needle, cast on 2 sts, rep from Row 1 until there are 8 BT with 6 sts in each triangle.

First Half Right Side Triangle (RT) (to form straight right edge)
Turn work to RS.
Row 1 (RS) K2, turn.
Row 2 Sl 1, p1.
Row 3 Sl 1, M1, ssk, turn.
Row 4 Sl 1, p2.
Row 5 Sl 1, M1, k1, ssk, turn.

Row 6 Sl 1, p3.

Row 7 Sl 1, M1, k2, ssk, turn.

Row 8 Sl 1, p4.

Row 9 Sl 1, M1, k3, ssk, do not turn.

Left Leaning Rectangle

Row 1 Pick up and k 6 sts down edge of BT (12 sts on RH needle), turn.

Row 2 Sl 1, p5, turn.

Row 3 Sl 1, k4, ssk, turn.

Row 4 Sl 1, p5, turn. Cont forming a rectangle as established until all triangle sts are used up. Rep until 7 rectangles are formed across, end with RS, do not turn.

Left Side Triangle (LT)

Row 1(RS) Pick up and k 6 sts down edge of last triangle, turn.

Row 2 Sl 1, p5, turn.

Row 3 Sl 1, k3, k2tog.

Row 4 Sl 1, p4, turn.

Row 5 Sl 1, k2, k2tog.

Row 6 Sl 1, p3, turn. Cont as established until 1 st rem, turn.

Right Leaning Rectangle

Row 1(WS) Sl rem st to RH needle, pick up and p 5 sts down LT just worked, turn.

Next row Sl 1, k5.

Next row Sl 1, p4, p2tog, turn.

Next row Sl 1, k5.

Next row Sl 1, p4, p2tog, turn. Cont as established until all sts from first rectangle are used up, end with WS. Pick up

and k 6 sts down 2nd rectangle. Cont as established. Work rectangles and triangles as indicated on diagram, end with a LT.

Finishing Triangles (FT) (WS)

Row 1 Sl rem st to RH needle, pick up and p 6 sts down LT, turn.

Next row Sl 1, k4, k2tog.

Next row Sl 1, p4, p2tog, turn.

Next row Sl 1, k3, k2tog.

Next row Sl 1, p3, p2tog, turn.

Next row Sl 1, k2, k2tog.

Next row Sl 1, p2, p2tog, turn.

Next row Sl 1, k1, k2tog.

Next row Sl 1, p1, p2tog, turn.

Next row Sl 1, k2tog.

Next row Sl 1, p2tog, turn.

Next row Ssk.

Next row P2tog, do not turn. With rem st on RH needle, pick up and p 6 sts down next rectangle. Cont working FT as before until all sts are worked. Pull yarn through last st at end.

BACK

Work as for Front.

FINISHING

Stretch pieces to measurements and pin down. Steam block with damp cotton cloth, let dry. With tapestry needle, and RS of front and back tog, backstitch 3 sides. Turn to RS. Insert pillow form. Sew rem side.

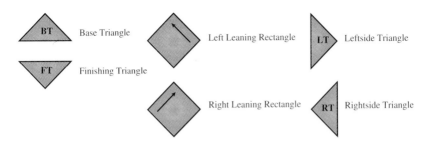

BT Base Triangle

FT Finishing Triangle

Left Leaning Rectangle

Right Leaning Rectangle

LT Leftside Triangle

RT Rightside Triangle

ENTRELAC PILLOW DIAGRAM

CHAIR PILLOW

Please be seated

For Intermediate Knitters

A perfect accent for your favorite chair. This charming pillow, designed by Kristin Nicholas, sports its own detachable mini-cushion. Embroidery and duplicate stitch embellish the picture. Choose a lively fabric to back the colorful pillow top.

KNITTED MEASUREMENTS
21" x 11"/53.5cm x 28cm without mitered edging

MATERIALS
■ 2 1¾oz/50g hanks (each approx 95yds/87m) of Classic Elite *Tapestry* (wool/mohair④) in #2296 daffodil (A)
■ 3 hanks in #2295 purple (B)
■ 1 hank each in #2205 pink (C), #2272 green (D)
■ One pair size 5 (3.75mm) needles
■ Three size 5 (3.75mm) circular needles, 29"/74cm long, *or size to obtain gauge*
■ 4 Stitch markers
■ Tapestry needle (for embroidery)
■ Fabric for backing 17" x 22"/43cm x 56cm
■ Fabric to make pillow form 12" x 43"/30.5cm x 109cm
■ Fiberfill

GAUGE
21 sts and 24 rows to 4"/10cm over St st and chart pat, using size 5 (3.75mm) needles. *Take time to check gauge.*

STITCHES USED

Border Stripe pat
With C, p 2 rnds. With D, k 1 rnd, p 1 rnd.

With B, k 1 rnd, p 2 rnds. Bind off purlwise with B.

FRONT
With size 5 (3.75mm) needles and A, cast on 60 sts. Work foll chart, stranding A and B behind throughout on rows 7-126 to create a thick fabric. When row 132 of chart is complete, bind off all sts with A.

EMBROIDERY
With tapestry needle and single strand C, stem stitch outline as indicated on chart. With double strand of D, work small straight sts randomly on background of entire pillow.

FINISHING
With RS facing, size 5 (3.75mm) circular needle and C, *pick up and k 56 sts at bottom edge of pillow, pick up corner st (c-st), mark c-st, pick up every 2nd and 3rd row at side of pillow, pick up c-st, mark c-st*; using 2nd circular needle rep between *'s once. With 3rd circular needle, work in Border stripe pat, AT SAME TIME, miter the corners every 2nd row as foll: work to st before marked c-st, M1, k c-st, M1. Rep at each corner. Cut backing fabric in half (8" x 22"/21.5cm x 56cm). Press ¼"/0.5cm to WS twice on side seam edges (omitting center edge) at each piece and hem. Press ½"/1.25cm, then 1"/2.5cm to WS at center edge of each piece and hem. Sew both pieces to back of pillow inside border overlapping each other at center by 2"/5cm.

Chair Cushion
With size 5 (3.75mm) needles and D, cast

on 38 sts. Work in St st for 30 rows, AT SAME TIME dec 1 st each end alternately every 3rd and 4th row until 22 sts rem. Bind off. Work French knot embroidery in A randomly on entire flap. With size 5 (3.75mm) circular needle and C, *Pick up and k 38 sts at bottom edge of flap, 26 sts at side of flap, 22 sts at top of flap and 26 sts at other side of flap—112 sts. Purl 2 rnds, working with 2 circular needles. Bind off purlwise. Using one strand of D, tie flap to chair motif, use photo as guide. With RS tog, fold pillow form fabric in half. Sew with ½"/1.25cm seam leaving opening. Turn RS out, stuff with fiberfill. Sew opening closed. Insert form into pillow.

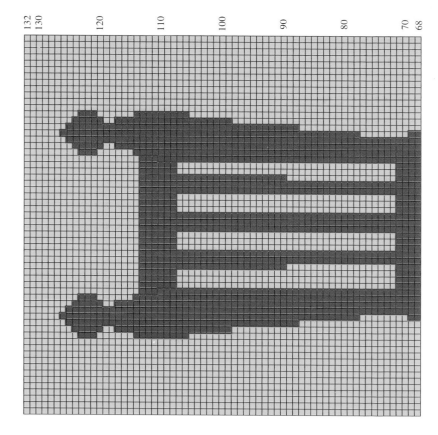

Color key

- ☐ Daffodil (A)
- ■ Purple (B)
- ■ Pink (C)

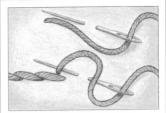

Stem Stitch

Bring needle up on edge of area to be outlined. Insert it a short distance to the right at an angle and pull it through, emerging at the midpoint of the previous stitch. Work left to right, keeping the thread below the needle.

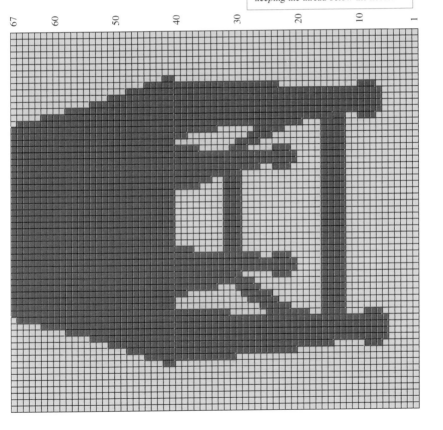

Home on the range...these pillows designed by Teva Durham feature bands of pattern alternating with slip stitch, textured knitting and intarsia. One has a ribbed flange; the other is folded into a rectangle and fringed.

KNITTED MEASUREMENTS

Square Pillow

14" x 14"/35.5cm x 35.5cm square with additional 3"/7.5cm flanged edge

Rectangular Pillow

18"/46cm wide and 26"/66cm long folded in half to form 18" x 13"/46cm x 33cm rectangle

MATERIALS

Square Pillow

■ 5 1¾oz/50g skeins (each approx 110yd/100m) of Cleckheaton *Machine Wash 8-ply Crepe* by Plymouth Yarns (wool③) in #1863 cream (A)

■ 1 skein each in #1960 copper (B), #1965 light green (C), #1547 dark teal (D), #1871 light teal (E), #1847 brown (F)

■ One size 3 (3.25mm) circular needle, 36"/92cm long

■ Pillow form 14" x 14"/35.5cm x 35.5cm square

Rectangular Pillow

■ 2 1¾oz/50g skeins (each approx 110yd/100m) of Cleckheaton *Machine Wash 8-ply Crepe* by Plymouth Yarns (wool③) in #1863 cream (A)

■ 1 skein each in #1960 copper (B), #1965 light green (C), #1547 dark teal (D), #1871 light teal (E), #1847 brown (F)

■ 14 recycled glass buttons, available

from One World Button Supply Co.

■ Pillow form 18" x 13"/46cm x 33cm rectangle

■ Size 6/G (4.5mm) crochet hook (for fringe)

Both versions

■ One pair size 7 (4.5mm) needles, *or size to obtain gauge.*

■ Tapestry needle

GAUGE

22 sts and 30 rows to 4"/10cm over St st with larger needles. *Take time to check gauge.*

SQUARE PILLOW

FRONT

With A, cast on 82 sts. Keeping first and last st as selvage st (k every row), work 11 rows of Purl Diamond chart with A. Work 7 rows of Band chart 1. Work 10 rows of Slip chart with C. Work 7 rows of Band chart 2. Work 27 rows of Intarsia chart. Work 7 rows Band chart 2. Work 10 rows Slip chart with C. Work 7 rows Band chart 1. Work 11 rows of Purl diamond chart with A. Bind off with A.

FLANGE

With circular needle and A, beg at a corner on front piece, pick up and k 2 sts in each corner and 82 sts along each side—336 sts. Join and work in k2, p2 rib as foll: *k2 (corner sts), [k2, p2] 20 times, k2; rep from * around. Cont as established, inc 1 st each side of 2 corner stitches (working inc sts into k2, p2 rib and keeping corner sts as k2) every other row, until flange measures 3"/7.5cm. Bind off in rib.

BACK

With A, cast on 82 sts and work Slip chart for 14"/35.5 cm. Bind off.

FINISHING

Sew three sides of back piece to front piece beneath flange. Insert pillow form. Sew last side.

RECTANGULAR PILLOW

Work in one piece.

With A, cast on 100 sts. **Work 11 rows Purl diamond chart. Work 7 rows Band chart 1. Work 20 rows Slip Stripe Chart.

Work 7 rows Band chart 1. Rep from ** 3 times more. Bind off.

FINISHING

Cut strands of every color 8"/20cm long for fringe. Attach along sides of piece, using color to match each stripe. Fold in half, matching cast-on and bind-off edges. Sew side seam. Insert pillow form. Sew 7 buttons on each side inside of fringe through both layers.

Stitch key

☐ k on RS, p on WS

⊟ p on RS, k on WS

Ⓤ slip wyif on RS, slip wyib on WS in color indicated

SLIP CHART

12-st rep

PURL DIAMOND

16-st rep

SLIP STRIPE CHART

16-st rep

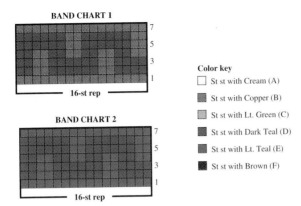

BAND CHART 1

7
5
3
1

— 16-st rep —

BAND CHART 2

7
5
3
1

— 16-st rep —

Color key

☐ St st with Cream (A)

St st with Copper (B)

St st with Lt. Green (C)

St st with Dark Teal (D)

St st with Lt. Teal (E)

St st with Brown (F)

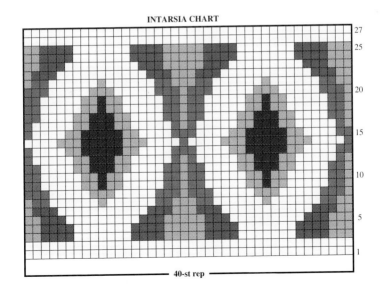

INTARSIA CHART

27
25

20

15

10

5

1

— 40-st rep —

RUCHED VELVET PILLOW

Opulent color and sumptuous texture

For Intermediate Knitters

This elegant pillow, designed by Jacquelyn Smyth, evokes the rich luxury of boudoir upholstery. The pillow top is knit in-the-round using increases and decreases to create the gathered effect.

KNITTED MEASUREMENTS
18" x 18"/46cm x 46cm

MATERIALS
■ 6 1¾oz/50g balls (each approx 110yds/100m) of Skacel Collection *Czarina* (acrylic/nylon⑤) in #003 red
■ Two size 6 (4mm) circular needles, 29"/74cm long *or size to obtain gauge*
■ 8 Stitch markers
■ 1 Row marker
■ Tapestry needle
■ 18" x 18"/46cm x 46cm pillow form
■ Matching shank buttons, one 2¼"/5.5cm and one 1"/25mm

GAUGE
16 sts and 26 rows to 4"/10cm over St st, using size 6 (4mm) needles. *Take time to check gauge.*

STITCHES USED:

Stockinette stitch (St st)
When worked in rows: K on RS, P on WS.
When worked circular: K every rnd.

FRONT

Center Square
Cast on 20 sts. Working back and forth on circular needle, work in St st for 4"/10cm, end with a WS row. Bind off.

First Border
With RS facing and first circular needle,

pick up and k 20 sts along one side of square, place marker (pm), pick up and k 1 corner st (c-st), pm; rep between *'s once more, with 2nd circular needle rep between *'s twice—84 sts. Join, mark beg of rnd. Cont working with 2 circular needles.

Rnd 1 (inc rnd) *[Inc 1 st in next st, k1] 9 times, k1, inc 1 st in next st, sl marker, k c-st, sl marker*; rep between *'s 3 times more—124 sts. Work in St st for 14 rnds, AT SAME TIME, inc 1 st before and after marked c-st on every rnd—236 sts.

Next (Dec) rnd *K1, [k2tog, k1] 19 times, sl marker, k c-st, sl marker*; rep between *'s 3 times more—160 sts.

Next rnd *K1, bind off tightly to 1 st before marker, k1, sl marker, k c-st, sl marker*; rep between *'s 3 times more—12 sts.

Second Border
Use one circular needle only.

Next rnd *Inc 1 in next st, pick up and k 45 sts along bound-off sts from previous rnd, inc 1 in next st, sl marker, k c-st, sl marker*; rep between *'s 3 times more—200 sts.

Next (Inc) rnd *[Inc 1 in next st, k2] 16 times, inc 1 in next st, sl marker, k c-st, sl marker*; rep between *'s 3 times more—268 sts. Work in St st for 14 rnds, AT SAME TIME, inc 1 st before and after marked c-st on every rnd—380 sts.

Next (Dec) rnd *K1, [k2tog, k2] 10 times, [k2tog, k1] 4 times, [k2, k2tog] 10 times, k1, sl marker, k c-st, sl marker*; rep between *'s 3 times more—284 sts.

Next rnd *K1, bind off tightly to 1 st before marker, k1, sl marker, k c-st, sl marker*; rep between *'s 3 times more—12 sts.

Third Border

Next rnd *Inc 1 in next st, pick up and k 69 sts along bound-off sts from previous rnd, inc 1 in next st, sl marker, k c-st, sl marker*; rep between *'s 3 times more—296 sts.

Next (Inc) rnd *[Inc 1 in next st, k2] 24 times, inc 1 in next st, sl marker, k c-st, sl marker*; rep between *'s 3 times more—396 sts. Work in St st for 14 rnds, AT SAME TIME, inc 1 st before and after marked c-st on every rnd—508 sts.

Next (Dec) rnd *K1, [k2tog, k2] 15 times, k1, k2tog, k1, [k2, k2tog] 15 times, k1, sl marker, k c-st, sl marker*; rep between *'s 3 times more—384 sts. Bind off all sts.

BACK

Cast on 72 sts. Work back and forth with circular needle in St st for 18"/46cm, end with a WS row. Bind off.

FINISHING

With tapestry needle and WS of front and back tog, backstitch 3 sides, one st in from edge. Insert pillow form. Place large button inside pillow under center 4"/10cm square on front. Gather fabric over button and tie with a strand of yarn. With tapestry needle and yarn, thread through shank of button and pull through pillow form to center back and thread through a smaller shank button. Thread through shank several times and secure.

WORKING WITH CHENILLE

■ *Don't be surprised by the needle size. Chenille takes a smaller needle than usually required for similar weight yarns. This creates a dense fabric and keeps the stitches in check, giving them less leeway to "worm" out of place into an uneven, loopy appearance.*

■ *Avoid over-twisting. Twisting crushes the pile and may cause stitches to curl out of place. The British method of knitting (throwing or casting yarn over the needle with the right hand) twists the yarn to a greater extent than the Continental, making the latter better suited to working with chenille. British-style knitters should guide the yarn over the needle without any extra twists.*

■ *Accustom yourself to yarn with very little "give." Work each stitch with a slight firmness to prevent any slack, but don't pull too tight as chenille may break when stretched.*

■ *Protect the pile surface from picking up fuzz and lint. As you're knitting, keep the ball in a sandwich bag with a twist-tie at the top, or a resealable bag, leaving a small opening for the working yarn. An alternate way to protect the surface and control the feed of the yarn is with a nylon spool protector (see Working with Ribbon Yarns on page 59).*

BROCADE BOLSTERS
Elegant accents in luxury yarns

For Intermediate Knitters

Bolsters inspired by fine French furnishings, designed by Teva Durham. A simple slip stitch in chenille and ribbon yarns imitates rich brocade. Covers are knit in-the-round and gathered at both ends, then trimmed with purchased tassels.

KNITTED MEASUREMENTS

6"/15cm diameter x 14"/35.5 cm long

MATERIALS

Blue Pillow

■ 5 1¾oz/50g skeins (each approx 61yd/56m) of Muench *Touch Me* (viscose/wool⑤) in #3606 blue (A)

■ 2 1¾oz/50g skeins (each approx 108yd/100m) of Gedifra/Muench *Minerva* (polymid③) in #1062 blue (B)

Olive Pillow

■ 5 1¾oz/50g skeins (each approx 61yd/56m) of Muench *Touch Me* (viscose/wool⑤) in #3610 olive (A)

■ 2 1¾oz/50g skeins (each approx 108yd/100m) of Gedifra/Muench *Minerva* (polymid③) in #1061 olive (B)

Both versions

■ One pair size 5 (3.75mm) circular needle 18"/46cm long, *or size to obtain gauge*

■ Safety pin

■ Pillow form 6"/15cm diameter x 14"/35.5cm long

■ 2 tassels 3½"/9cm long

GAUGE

16 sts and 18 rows to 4"/10cm over Slip stitch lattice pat with size 5 (3.75mm) needle. *Take time to check gauge.*

Notes 1 Pillow is knit in the round as a tube.

2 Motifs at end and beg of rounds will have an extra stitch of B where necessary to carry the pattern full circle; due to the quality of the ribbon yarn this will not be noticable.

STITCH GLOSSARY

Slip Stitch Lattice pat (over multiple of 6 sts)

Rnd 1 With B, *k3, sl 3 wyif; rep from * to end.

Rnd 2 With B, *k3, sl 3 wyif; rep from * to end.

Rnd 3 K1 with B, with A k to end of rnd.

Rnds 4 and 5 K all sts with A.

Rnd 6 K with A to last st, k1 with B.

Rnd 7 With B, *sl 3 wyif, k1, insert RH needle under 2 strands below (floats from sl 3 wyif) and k into st on LH needle, k1; rep from * to end.

Rnd 8 With B, *sl 3 wyif, k3; rep from * to end.

Rnds 9 and 12 K with A.

Rnd 13 With B, *k1, insert RH needle under 2 strands below (floats from sl 3 wyif) and k into st on LH needle, k1, sl 3 wyif; rep from * to end.

Rnd 14 With B, *k3, sl 3 wyif; rep from * to end.

Rep rnds 3-14 for Slip st lattice pat.

ROLL PILLOW

With A and circular needle, cast on 78 sts. Work back and forth as if on straight needles in St st for 3 rows.

Next row (WS) Knit (turning ridge). Work 3 rows St st. With RS facing, join rnd and work next rnd as foll: Fold hem and start with first st on right, *place loop of cast-on edge on LH needle, k it tog with st; rep from * to end, pm. K every rnd until piece measures 4"/10cm. P1 rnd. Work in Slip st lattice pat, working rnds 1-14 once, then rep rnds 3-14 10 times, working last 2 rnds as foll:

Rnd 13 With B, *k1, insert RH needle under 2 strands below (floats from sl 3 wyif) and k into st on LH needle, k1, sl 3 wyib; rep from * to end.

Rnd 14 With B, *k3, sl 3 wyib; rep from * to end. Piece measures 19"/48cm from beg. With A, p1 rnd. Work in St st for 4"/10cm. Turn, and work back and forth in St st for 3 rows.

Next row (RS) Purl. Work 3 rows St st. Bind off.

FINISHING

Sew bound-off hem under. Insert pillow form, positioning purl ridges at ends of roll. Cut a 44"/112cm length of A and fold in half, thread into safety pin. Run doubled yarn through hem casing. Holding yarn at both sides of casing, pull to gather. Wrap yarn ends tightly around outside of puckered hem to form rosette. Secure yarn ends, and pull through to middle of rosette. Sew purchased tassel to inside of rosette.

WORKING WITH RIBBON YARNS

■ *Place a nylon spool protector (a tube of netting) or a tube cut from an old stocking around your ball of ribbon so it won't unwind too fast. Slinky ribbon yarns slide off the ball very easily causing tangles or knots.*

■ *Avoid pulling the ribbon. Keep a light hold as ribbons have a great deal of stretch and can distort when pulled.*

■ *As with chenille, avoid over-twisting. A ribbon will have the best appearance when it lays flat.*

■ *Clean your hands before knitting. Natural oils may stain or stiffen the rayon fiber used in most ribbons and some chenilles.*

■ *Use non-slip needles. Needles of bamboo or wood will give you more control when working with slippery yarns.*

NAVAJO PILLOWS

Southwest flavor in a spicy palette

For Intermediate Knitters

Inspired by Native American woven blankets, these fulled Navajo pillows were designed by Gail Diven. Knit in Icelandic wool, the pillow tops are crocheted to felt backings for easy finishing.

KNITTED MEASUREMENTS
(after fulling)

Rectangular Pillow
18"/46cm wide x 12"/30.5cm long

Square Pillow
12" x 12"/30.5cm x 30.5cm

MATERIALS

Rectangular Pillow
■ 1 1¾oz/50g ball (each approx 109yd/100m) of Reynolds *Lite Lopi* (wool④) each in #0056 grey (A), #0051 off-white (B), #0434 red (C), #0264 gold (D) and #0059 black (E)

Square Pillow
■ 1 1¾oz/50g ball (each approx 109yd/100m) of Reynolds *Lite Lopi* (wool④) each in #0056 grey (A), #0051 off-white (B), #0423 teal (C), #0264 gold (D) and #0059 black (E)

Both versions
■ One pair size 8 (5mm) needles *or size to obtain gauge*
■ Bobbins
■ Size 6 steel (1.5mm) crochet hook
■ Non-raveling wool fabric (felt, melton, etc.) for backing **Rectangular Pillow:** 12" x 18"/30.5cm x 46cm, **Square Pillow:** 12" x 12"/30.5cm x 30.5cm
■ Pillow form **Rectangular Pillow:** 12" x 18"/ 30.5cm x 46cm, **Square Pillow:** 12" x 12"/30.5cm x 30.5cm

GAUGE
17 sts and 22 rows to 4"/10cm (before fulling) over St st, using size 8 (5mm) needles. *Take time to check gauge.*

Notes 1 Use separate bobbins for large blocks of color or strand colors across the back for Fair Isle sections.

2 When changing colors, twist yarns around each other on WS to avoid holes.

3 Fulled measurements may vary. Measure carefully after fulling and adjust backing and pillow form measurements if necessary.

FRONT

Rectangular Pillow
With size 8 (5mm) needles and A, cast on 82 sts.
Beg Rectangular Pillow Chart: Row 1 (RS)
Work sts 1-52, then sts 1-30. Cont as established through chart row 74. Bind off with A.

Square Pillow
With size 8 (5mm) needles and C, cast on 56 sts. Working Square Pillow chart, work rows 1-22, then rows 3-22 twice more, then rows 23-34. There are a total of 74 rows. Bind off with C.

FINISHING
Weave in loose ends.

Fulling
Place pieces in mesh sack in washing machine, using hot cycle. Rinse cold. Place in dryer for added shrinkage. With steam iron and pressing cloth, press to measurements. Cut backing fabric same size as fulled front. With WS of backing and front tog, using crochet hook and E, work 1 rnd sc along 3 sides, working 3 sc in corners. Insert pillow form. Crochet rem side closed, join. Ch 1, from RS sl st into center of each sc. Fasten off.

Color key

- Grey (A)
- Off-White (B)
- Red (C)
- Gold (D)
- Black (E)

RECTANGULAR PILLOW

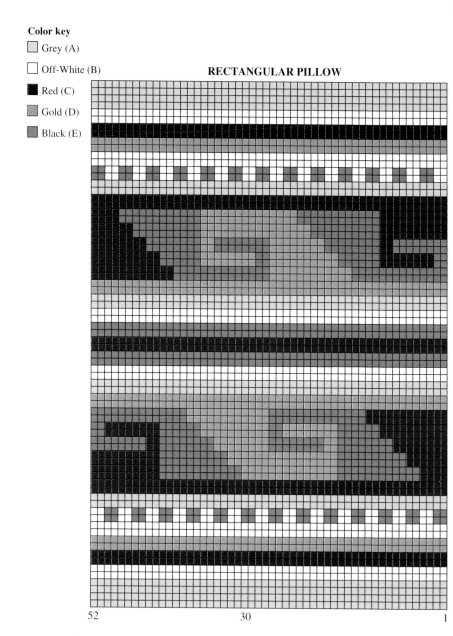

52   30   1

Color key

- ☐ Grey (A)
- ☐ Off-White (B)
- ■ Teal (C)
- ▨ Gold (D)
- ▨ Black (E)

SQUARE PILLOW

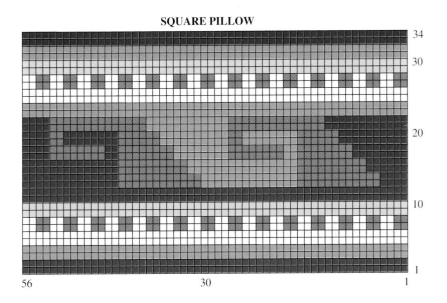

For Intermediate Knitters

Conversation-piece chenille cubes designed by Abigail Liles. Each cube is worked with yarn held double and woven-type stitch patterns for plush velvet appeal.

KNITTED MEASUREMENTS
8"/20cm square cube

MATERIALS
- 3 1.4oz/40g skeins (each approx 87yd/80m) Lion Brand *Chenille Sensations* (acrylic⑤) each in #142 mulberry (A) and #140 raspberry (B)
- 2 skeins in #134 brick (C)
- One pair size 9 (5.5mm) needles *or size to obtain gauge*
- Fiberfill

GAUGE
- 17 sts and 20 rows to 4"/10cm using size 9 (5.5mm) needles over Purl twist pat with 2 strands of A held tog.
- 18 sts and 26 rows to 4"/10cm using size 9 (5.5mm) needles over Ridge st pat with 2 strands of B held tog.
- 14 sts and 28 rows to 4"/10cm using size 9 (5.5mm) needles over Woven st pat with 2 strands of C held tog. *Take time to check gauge.*

STITCHES USED

Purl Twist pat (even number of sts)
Rows 1 and 3 (RS) Knit.
Row 2 *P2tog, do not sl sts from LH needle, p1 in first st, sl both sts to RH needle; rep from * to end.

Row 4 P1, rep from * of row 2; end p1.
Rep rows 1-4 for Purl twist pat.

Ridge St pat (even number of sts)
Row 1 Knit.
Row 2 K2tog across row.
Row 3 K into the front and back of each st.
Row 4 Purl.
Rep rows 1-4 for Ridge st pat.

Woven St pat (even number of sts)
Rows 1 and 3 (WS) Purl.
Row 2 K1, *sl 1 wyif, k1; rep from *, end k1.
Row 4 K1, *k1, sl 1 wyif; rep from *, end k1.
Rep rows 1-4 for Woven st pat.

PILLOW

Mulberry square (make 2)
With size 9 (5.5mm) needles and 2 strands of A held tog, cast on 34 sts. Work in Purl twist pat for 8"/20cm. Bind off.

Raspberry Square (make 2)
With size 9 (5.5mm) needles and 2 strands of B held tog, cast on 36 sts. Work in Ridge st pat for 8"/20cm. Bind off.

Brick Square (make 2)
With size 9 (5.5mm) needles and 2 strands of C held tog, cast on 28 sts. Work in Woven st pat for 8"/20cm. Bind off.

FINISHING
Sew pieces tog to form a cube, leaving one seam open. Stuff pillow and sew rem side closed.

LACE OVERLAY

Delicate dress-up for lovers of lace

Fine lace mohair makes a perfect top for a simple cotton batiste pillow. E. J. Slayton designed this dainty knit-in-the-round lace overlay; the added borders are knit side-to-side.

KNITTED MEASUREMENTS

18" x 18"/46cm x 46cm without edging

MATERIALS

- 1 .87oz/25g ball (each approx 268yds/245m) of Filatura Di Crosa *Kid Mohair* (mohair/nylon①) in #384 light blue
- Size 6 (4mm) circular needles 16"/42cm and 24"/60cm long *or size to obtain gauge*
- One set (5) size 6 (4mm) double pointed needles (dpn)
- Stitch markers
- Sewing needle and matching thread
- Matching fabric for pillow cover 19" x 37"/48cm x 94cm
- Pillow form 18" x 18"/46cm x 46cm

GAUGE

11.5 sts and 22.5 rows to 4"/10cm over Chart pat (blocked), using size 6 (4mm) needles. *Take time to check gauge.*

Notes 1 Place marker after each chart repeat.
2 Change from dpn to circular needle when enough sts available and mark first st of each section.
3 Edging is worked back and forth in rows. Last st of edging is knitted tog with 1 st of pillow every other row; corners are shaped with short rows.

FRONT

With size 6 (4mm) dpn cast on 8 sts. Divide sts evenly on 4 dpn (2 sts on each needle). Join and place marker (pm) for beg of rnd.
Beg Chart pat: Rnd 1 Rep chart sts 4 times around. Cont in chart pat as established through chart rnd 51.
Note Change to circular needle when necessary and mark each of the 4 sections. There is a total of 208 sts. Do not break yarn.

EDGING

With RS of pillow facing, cast on 7 sts.
Foundation Row K4, yo, p2tog, k2tog (last st of edging tog with 1 st of pillow), turn.
Shaping corner with short rows:
Row 1 (WS) Sl 1, yo, p2tog, k2, yo twice, k2.
Row 2 K2, (k1, p1) in double yo, k2, turn.
Row 3 Sl 1, k1, yo twice, k2tog, yo twice, k2.
Row 4 K2, (k1, p1) in double yo, k1, (k1, p1) in double yo, k2, yo, p2tog, k2tog (last st of edging tog with 1 st of pillow), turn.

Row 5 Sl 1, yo, p2tog, k9.

Row 6 Bind off 5 sts, k3, turn.

Row 7 Sl 1, yo, k1, yo twice, k2.

Row 8 K2, k1 p1 into yo's, k2, yo, p2tog, k2tog, turn.

Row 9 Sl 1, yo, p2tog, k2, yo twice, k2tog, yo twice, k2.

Row 10 K2, k1 p1 into yo's, k1, k1 p1 into yo's, k2, yo, p2tog, k2tog, (last st of edging tog with 1 st of pillow), turn.

Row 11 Rep row 5.

Row 12 Bind off 5 sts, k3, yo, p2tog, k2tog, (last st of edging tog with 1 st of pillow).

Main Edging pat

Row 1 Sl 1, yo, p2tog, k2, yo twice, k2.

Row 2 K2, (k1, p1) in double yo, k2, yo, p2tog, k2tog (last st of edging tog with 1 st of pillow), turn.

Row 3 Sl 1, yo, p2tog, k2, yo twice, k2tog, yo twice, k2.

Row 4 K2, (k1 p1) in double yo, k1, (k1 p1) in double yo, k2, yo, p2tog, k2tog (last

st of edging tog with 1 st of pillow), turn.

Row 5 Sl 1, yo, p2tog, k9.

Row 6 Bind off 5 sts, k3, yo, p2tog, k2tog (last st of edging tog with 1 st of pillow), there are 7 sts on RH needle.

Rep last 6 rows for Main Edging pat until 2 sts before corner. Shape corner with short rows 1-10 as before. Rep between **'s around, ending last corner with row 5.

Next row Bind off 5 sts, weave rem sts to cast-on sts at beg of edging.

FINISHING

Steam block, pinning center part to 18"/46cm square. Let dry. With RS tog, fold pillow form fabric in half. Sew 3 sides with ½"/1.25cm seam. Insert pillow form. Sew final side. With sewing needle and matching thread, tack overlay to pillow.

LACE PAT

52 sts

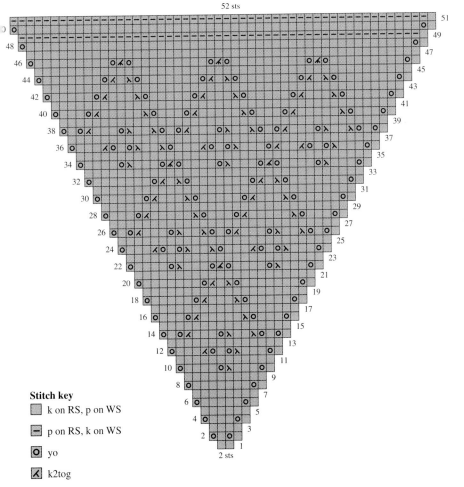

Stitch key

- ▢ k on RS, p on WS
- ⊟ p on RS, k on WS
- ☑ yo
- ◪ k2tog
- ◪ ssk
- ◪ k3tog

2 sts

OAK AND ACORN PILLOWS
Seasonal splendor all year long

Oak leaf intarsia pillows, designed by Sasha Kagan, feature welted ruffle or lace edgings, and buttoned backs. Tweed, chenille and silk yarns bring Autumn's rich colors and textures indoors.

KNITTED MEASUREMENTS

Ruffle Edge Pillow

18" x 18"/46cm x 46cm (without edging)

Lace Edge Pillow

18" x 21"/46cm x 53cm (without edging)

MATERIALS

Ruffle Edge Pillow

■ 4 1¾oz/50g skeins (each approx 110yd/100m) Rowan *DK Tweed* (wool③) in #853 brown tweed (MC)

■ 2 1¾oz/50g skeins (each approx 126yd/115m) *Designer DK* (wool③) in #663 rust (A)

■ 1 .88oz/25g skein (each approx 74yd/67m) *Kid Silk* (mohair/silk③) in #971 orange (B)

■ 1 .88oz/25g skein (each approx 110yd/100m) of *Donegal Lambswool Tweed* (held double) (wool②) each in #485 dark green (C), #479 cinnamon (D), and #482 teal (E)

■ Pillow form 18" x 18"/46cm x 46cm

Lace Edge Pillow

■ 4 1¾oz/50g skeins of *DK Tweed* in #850 beige tweed (MC)

■ 2 1¾oz/50g skeins of *Designer DK* in #639 olive (A)

■ 1 .88oz/25g skein of *Kid Silk* in #989 gold (B)

■ 1 .88oz/25g skein of *Donegal Lambswool Tweed* (held double) in #483 brick red (C)

■ 1 1¾oz/50g skeins (each approx 176yd/160m) of *Fine Cotton Chenille* (cotton/polyester②) each in #409 plum (D), #406 robin (E)

■ Pillow form 18" x 21"/46cm x 53cm

Both versions

■ One pair each sizes 5 and 6 (3.75 and 4mm) needles *or size to obtain gauge*

■ Bobbins

■ Tapestry needle

■ Five buttons, ½"/13mm

GAUGES

■ 22 sts and 30 rows to 4"/10cm over St st and MC using size 5 (3.75mm) needles.

■ 24 sts and 29 rows to 4"/10cm over St st and chart pat using size 5 (3.75mm) needles. *Take time to check gauges.*

Notes I Use double strand of *Donegal Lambswool Tweed* throughout.

2 Use separate bobbins for chart motifs.

3 Carry MC loosely across WS of work when not in use.

4 When changing colors, twist yarns around each other on WS to avoid holes.

Twisted Rib (over an even number of sts)

Row 1 (RS) *K1tbl, p1; rep from * to end.
Rep row 1 for twisted rib.

RUFFLE EDGE PILLOW

FRONT

With size 5 (3.75mm) needles and MC,
cast on 106 sts.

Beg Chart: Row 1 (RS) Working in St st,
work 53-st rep of chart twice. Cont as
established through chart row 50. Rep chart
rows 1-50 once more, then work rows 1-28
once (128 rows). Bind off with MC.

BACK (worked in 2 sections)

Section 1

With size 5 (3.75mm) needles and MC, cast
on 100 sts. Work in St st for 8¼"/21cm, end
with a WS row.

Buttonband

Work in twisted rib for 1½"/4cm, end
with a WS row. Bind off in rib. Place
markers for 5 buttons along center of rib
band as foll: the first and last at 2"/5cm
in from each side and 3 others spaced
evenly between.

Section 2

Work as for section 1 until rib measures
¾"/2cm. Work 5 buttonholes opposite
markers as foll: bind off 2 sts for each buttonhole. On next row, cast on 2 sts over
bound-off sts. Complete as for buttonband.

FINISHING

With RS of both back sections facing, and
buttonhole band above buttonband, sew
rib tog at sides. Block pieces to measurements. With tapestry needle and RS of
front and back tog, backstitch all 4 sides.
Turn to RS.

WELTED RUFFLE EDGING

With size 6 (4mm) needles and A, cast
on 13 sts.

Row 1 K13.

Row 2 P10, turn.

Row 3 K10.

Row 4 P10, k3.

Row 5 K3, p10.

Row 6 K10, turn.

Row 7 P10.

Row 8 K13.

Rep rows 1-8 for pat until short
(garter st) edge fits around pillow,
end with a row 7. Bind off knitwise.
Using tapestry needle, sl st short
(garter st) edge in place. Sew on
buttons. Insert pillow form.

LACE EDGE PILLOW

FRONT

With size 5 (3.75mm) needles and MC, cast on 106 sts.

Beg Chart: Row I (RS) Working in St st, work 53-st rep of chart twice. Cont as established through chart row 50. Rep chart rows 1-50 twice more (150 rows). With MC work 3 rows in St st. Bind off purlwise.

BACK (worked in 2 sections)

Section I

With size 5 (3.75mm) needles and MC, cast on 100 sts. Work in St st for 9¾"/24.5cm, end with a WS row.

BUTTONBAND

Work in twisted rib for 1½"/4cm, end with a WS row. Bind off in rib. Place markers for 5 buttons along center of rib band as foll: the first and last at 2"/5cm in from each side and 3 others spaced evenly between.

Section 2

Work as for Ruffle Edge Pillow.

FINISHING

Work as for Ruffle Edge Pillow.

OAK LEAF EDGING

With size 5 (3.75mm) needles and A, cast on 10 sts.

Foundation Row Knit.

Row I (RS) Sl 1, k2, yo, k2tog, [yo twice, k2tog] twice, k1.

Row 2 Sl 1, [k1, in double yo work k1, p1] twice, k2, yo, k2tog, k1.

Row 3 Sl 1, k2, yo, k2tog, k2, [yo twice, k2tog] twice, k1.

Row 4 Sl 1, [k1, in double yo work k1, p1] twice, k4, yo, k2tog, k1.

Row 5 Sl 1, k2, yo, k2tog, k4 [yo twice, k2tog] twice, k1.

Row 6 Sl 1, [k1, in double yo work k1, p1] twice, k6, yo, k2tog, k1.

Row 7 Sl 1, k2, yo, k2tog, k6, [yo twice, k2tog] twice, k1.

Row 8 Sl 1, [k1, in double yo work k1, p1] twice, k8, yo, k2tog, k1.

Row 9 Sl 1, k2, yo, k2tog, k8, [yo twice, k2tog] twice, k1.

Row 10 Sl 1, [k1, in double yo work k1, p1] twice, k10, yo, k2tog, k1.

Row 11 Sl 1, k2, yo, k2tog, k15.

Row 12 Bind off 10 sts, k6, yo, k2tog, k1. Rep rows 1-12 until straight side of edging fits around pillow, end with a row 12. Bind off. Complete as for Ruffle Edge Pillow.

Color key

- Brown Tweed (MC)
- Rust (A)
- Orange (B)
- Dark Green (C)
- Cinnamon (D)
- Teal (E)

RUFFLE EDGE PILLOW

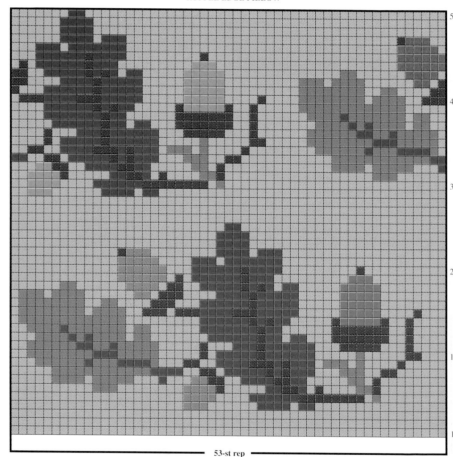

53-st rep

Color key

☐ Beige Tweed (MC)

■ Olive (A)

■ Gold (B)

■ Brick Red (C)

■ Plum (D)

■ Robin (E)

LACE EDGE PILLOW

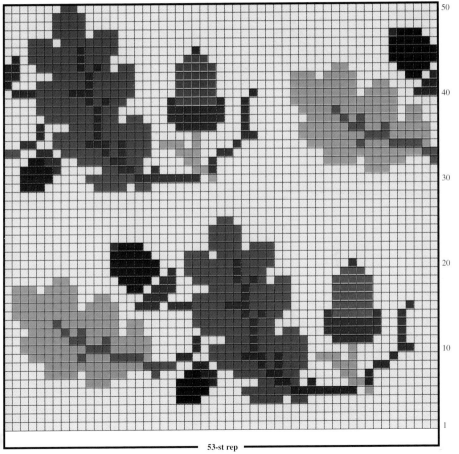

53-st rep

BEACH-HOUSE PILLOWS

Muted shades of sun, surf and sand

Refreshing trio of comfortable pillows in sun-washed colors, designed by Victoria Mayo. Checkered, striped and color-blocked pillows are embellished with purchased pom-pom trim.

KNITTED MEASUREMENTS
16" x 16"/40cm x 40cm

MATERIALS
Striped Pillow
- 2 1¾oz/50g balls (each approx 126yd/116m) of Phildar *Cabotage* (cotton/acrylic④) in #030 white (A)
- 1 ball each in #034 yellow (B), #033 blue (C), #036 green (D)
- 2yds/2m white pom-pom trim

Checkered Pillow
- 1 1¾oz/50g balls (each approx 126yd/116m) of Phildar *Cabotage* (cotton/acrylic④) in #030 white (A)
- 1 ball each in #034 yellow (B), #033 blue (C), #036 green (D)
- 2yds/2m white pom-pom trim

Color-blocked Pillow
- 2 1¾oz/50g balls (each approx 126yd/116m) of Phildar *Cabotage* (cotton/acrylic④) in #030 white (A)
- 1 ball each in #034 yellow (B), #033 blue (C), #036 green (D)
- 2yds/2m white pom-pom trim

All versions
- One pair size 7 (4.5mm) needles, *or size to obtain gauge*
- Tapestry needle
- Sewing needle
- White sewing thread
- Pillow form 16" x 16"/40cm x 40cm square

GAUGE
20 sts and 28 rows to 4"/10cm over St st using size 7 (4.5mm) needles. *Take time to check gauge.*

STRIPED PILLOW (make 2 pieces)
With size 7 (4.5mm) needles and A, cast on 80 sts. Work in St st and stripes as foll: 14 rows A, 14 rows D, 14 rows A, 14 rows B, 14 rows A, 14 rows C, 14 rows A, 14 rows D—piece measures 16"/40cm. Bind off.

CHECKERED PILLOW (make 2 pieces)
With size 7 (4.5mm) needles, cast on 20 sts C, 20 sts B, 20 sts A, 20 sts D—a total of 80 sts.
Next row (RS) K 20 sts D, 20 sts A, 20 sts B, 20 sts C. Cont in St st, matching colors, for a total of 28 rows.
Next row (RS) K 20 sts A, 20 sts B, 20 sts C, 20 sts D. Cont in St st, matching colors, for a total of 28 rows.
Next row (RS) K 20 sts B, 20 sts C, 20 sts D, 20 sts A. Cont in St st, matching colors, for a total of 28 rows.
Next row (RS) K 20 sts C, 20 sts D, 20 sts A, 20 sts B. Cont in St st, matching colors, for a total of 28 rows—piece measures 16"/40cm from beg. Bind off, matching colors.

COLOR-BLOCKED PILLOW (make 2 pieces)
With size 7 (4.5mm) needles cast on 40 sts with C and 40 sts with A. Work in St st, matching colors, for 56 rows.
Next row (RS) K 40 sts B, 40 sts D. Cont in St st, matching colors, for a total of 56 rows—piece measures 16"/40cm from beg. Bind off, matching colors.

FINISHING All versions
Block pieces. Pin or baste pom-pom trimming to WS of one piece. Sew with needle and thread. With yarn and tapestry needle, sew the two pieces together along three sides. Insert pillow form. Sem rem side.

Envelope-style pillows designed by Daria McGuire offer a ferocious mix of zebra and leopard prints. Contrast yarn laced through eyelet trim and horn buttons are ideal embellishments.

KNITTED MEASUREMENTS

16" x 16½"/40.5cm x 42cm (without edging)

MATERIALS

Makes both pillows

- 3 3½oz/100g balls (each approx 223yds/204m) of Patons *Classic Wool* (wool④) in #226 black (A)
- 2 balls in #206 rust (B)
- 1 ball each in #204 gold (C), #201 off-white (D), #231 brown (E)
- One pair size 7 (4.5mm) needles *or size to obtain gauge*
- Size 7 (4.5mm) circular needle, (used back and forth) 16"/40cm long
- Size G/6 (4.5mm) crochet hook
- Bobbins
- Tapestry needle
- Two pillow forms 16" x 16"/40.5cm x 40.5cm
- Two horn buttons, available from One World Button Supply Co.

GAUGE

20 sts and 27 rows to 4"/10cm over St st, using size 7 (4.5mm) needles. *Take time to check gauge.*

Notes I Use separate bobbins for chart motifs.

2 When changing colors, twist yarns around each other on WS to avoid holes.

3 Carry yarn loosely across WS of work when working smaller areas of color,

or duplicate st these areas afterwards.

ZEBRA PRINT PILLOW

FRONT

With size 7 (4.5mm) needles and A, cast on 80 sts. Work rows 1-104 of Zebra Print chart. Work 3 more rows in St st in A. K next row on WS for turning ridge. Work 4 more rows in St st. Bind off. Fold hem to WS at turning ridge and sew in place.

BACK

With size 7 (4.5mm) needles and A, cast on 80 sts. Work in St st for 108 rows, end with a WS row.

Beg Flap Turn Leopard Print chart upside down. Foll outline for Flap, work 51 rows, shape as indicated. Bind off rem 2 sts purlwise.

FINISHING

With RS of back and front tog, sew 2 sides and bottom seam. Turn to RS.

EDGING

With RS of front facing, size 7 (4.5mm) needles and A, pick up and k 80 sts evenly along side edge (omitting flap).

**Next row (WS) K2, *yo, k2tog, k1; rep from * to end.

Next row Purl. Bind off knitwise.** Work other side to match. With RS of front facing, and A, pick up and k 80 sts evenly along bottom edge and ends of side edging. Rep from ** to **.

FLAP EDGING

With RS of flap facing, circular needle (used back and forth) and A, pick up and k 10 sts along side edge, 48 sts from edge to point, 48 sts from point to edge and 10 sts along rem edge—116 sts. Rep from ** to **.

BUTTON LOOP

With WS of flap facing, crochet hook and B, beg 2 sts from peak center, ch 20. Fasten off, attach end 2 sts from center point on opposite side. Using tapestry needle, whipstitch double strand of B around entire outer edging through eyelets (using photo as guide). Rep for flap. Sew button in position. Insert pillow form.

LEOPARD PRINT PILLOW
FRONT

With size 7 (4.5mm) needles and B, cast on 80 sts. Work rows 1-104 of Leopard Print chart. Work 3 more rows in St st in B. K next row on WS for turning ridge. Work 4 more rows in St st. Bind off. Fold hem to WS at turning ridge and sew in place.

BACK

With size 7 (4.5mm) needles and B, cast on 80 sts. Work in St st for 108 rows, end with a WS row.

Beg Flap Turn Zebra Print chart upside down. Foll outline for Flap, work 51 rows, shape as indicated. Bind off rem 2 sts purlwise.

FINISHING

Work as for Zebra Print Pillow, using B for edging, A for Toggle-Loop and whipstitching.

Color key
■ Black (A)
□ Off-White (D)

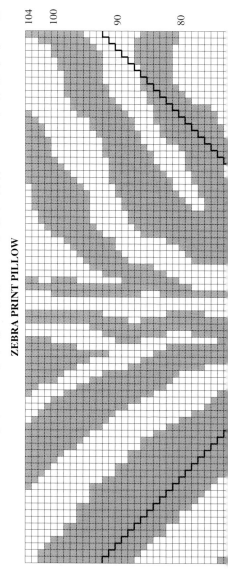

ZEBRA PRINT PILLOW

Color key

- ■ Rust (B)
- ☐ Gold (C)
- ■ Brown (E)

104 100 90 80 70 61

LEOPARD PRINT PILLOW

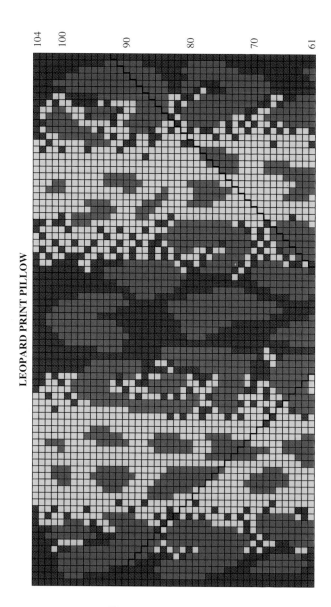

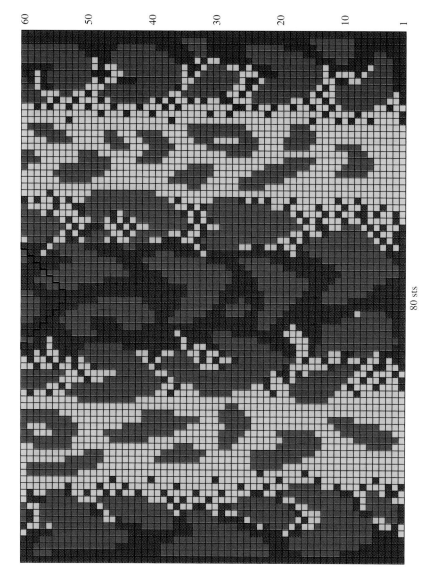

80 sts

For Intermediate Knitters

Lightly fulled and over-embroidered pillows designed by Rosemary Drysdale. Simple stripe and seed-stitched solid backgrounds are transformed with simple embroidery into a floral fantasy.

KNITTED MEASUREMENTS
(before fulling)

Stripe Pillow
19" x 19"/48cm x 48cm

Seed St Pillow
18" x 19"/46cm x 48cm

FINAL MEASUREMENTS
(after fulling)

Stripe Pillow
18" x 17"/47cm x 44.5cm

Seed St Pillow
17" x 17"/44.5cm x 44.5cm

MATERIALS

Stripe Pillow

- 6 1¾oz/50g skeins (each approx 77yds/70m) of Classic Elite *Poet* (wool/nylon⑤) in #5385 orange (MC)
- 1 skein #5351 gold (CC)
- 1 .88oz/25g skein (approx 69yd/62m) of *Cotton Sox* (cotton②) in #4952 grape (A), #4996 marigold (B), 4997 green (C)

Seed St Pillow

- 7 1¾/50g skeins (each approx 77yds/70m) of *Poet* (wool/nylon⑤) in #5302 lime (MC)
- 1 .88oz/25g skein (approx 69yd/62m) of *Cotton Sox* (cotton②) in #4952 grape (A), #4996 marigold (B), #4997 green (C), #4985 pumpkin (D)

Both versions

- One pair size 8 (5mm) needles *or size to obtain gauge*
- 4 buttons, ½"/13mm
- Tapestry needle
- Markers
- Pillow form 18" x 18"/46cm x 46cm

GAUGE (before washing)

- 15 sts and 22 rows to 4"/10cm over St st, using size 8 (5mm) needles
- 16 sts and 28 rows to 4"/10cm over Seed st, using size 8 (5mm) needles.
Take time to check gauge.

STITCHES USED

Stockinette Stitch (St st)
K the RS rows, p the WS rows.

Seed Stitch
Row 1 (RS) *K1, p1; rep from *.
Row 2 P the knit sts, and k the purl sts.
Rep row 2 for seed st.

STRIPE PILLOW

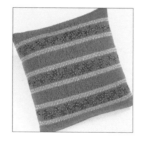

FRONT
With size 8 (5mm) needles and MC, cast on 72 sts. Work in St st and stripes as foll: 12 rows MC, [4 rows CC, 12 rows MC] 6 times—108 rows. Bind off with MC.

BACK (worked in 2 sections)

Section 1

With size 8 (5mm) needles and MC, cast on 66 sts. Work in St st for 9"/24cm, end with a WS row. Work in k1, p1 rib for 1"/2.5cm, end with a WS row. Bind off. Place marker on both sides, 2"/5cm down from bound-off edge.

Section 2

Work as for section 1 until rib measures ¼"/.5cm.

Next Buttonhole row Rib 11, [yo, k2tog, rib 12] 3 times, yo, k2tog, rib 11. Complete as for section 1.

FINISHING

Full front in washing machine using two cycles of hot wash and cold rinse, removing from machine frequently during 2nd cycle to measure. When piece approximates the "after" measurements, lay flat to dry. With tapestry needle and C, embroider 1 row herringbone st across CC stripes on front. Embroider flowers randomly in groups to MC stripes, using diagram and photo as guide. Sew center side seams of back, overlapping each other to markers. With tapestry needle and RS of front and back tog, backstitch tog. Turn to RS. Insert pillow form.

SEED ST PILLOW

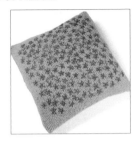

FRONT

With size 8 (5mm) needles and MC, cast on 72 sts. Work in Seed St until piece measures 19"/48cm, end with a WS row. Bind off in Seed st.

BACK (worked in 2 sections)

Section 1

With size 8 (5mm) needles and MC, cast on 66 sts. Work in St st for 8¾"/22cm, end with a WS row. Work in k1, p1 rib for 1"/2.5cm, end with a WS row. Bind off. Place marker on both sides, 2"/5cm down from bound-off edge.

Section 2

Work as for section 1 of Stripe Pillow.

FINISHING

Full front as for Stripe Pillow. Embroider flowers randomly in groups on front, using diagram and photo as a guide. Sew center side seams of back, overlapping each other to markers. With tapestry needle and RS of front and back tog, backstitch tog. Turn to RS. Insert pillow form.

- Lazy Daisy St, double strand
- Straight St & French Knot, single strand
- Straight St, double strand

- Straight St, single strand
- Straight St, double strand
- Lazy Daisy St & French Knot, double strand
- Lazy Daisy St, double strand

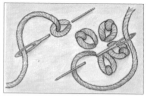

Lazy Daisy

I *Draw the needle up through the work. Insert the needle back next to where it just came out, and take a short stitch. Hold the yarn in place with your thumb, and with the needle point above the yarn, draw the needle through.*

2 *Insert the needle back into the fabric on the other side of the stitch, securing it with a bar.*

3 *Form each succeeding petal in the same way, always bringing the needle up into the center of the circle.*

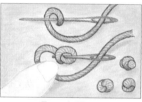

French Knot

Draw the needle up through the work, wrap the yarn once or twice around the needle, and hold yarn taut. Reinsert the needle at the closest point to where the yarn emerged, gently pulling it through to the back of the work.

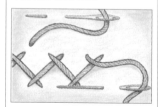

Herringbone Stitch

Working from left to right, bring the needle up, then across diagonally and take a short stitch back to the left. Bring the needle down diagonally and take a short stitch as shown.

SILK LAVENDER SACHETS

Indulge your senses in lavender and lace

Lace lavender sachets designed by Lila P. Chin will soothe restless minds and tired eyes. Knit in sumptuous silk yarn, they cover matching silk sachets filled with dried lavender.

KNITTED MEASUREMENTS

Sachet
4" x 4"/10cm x 10cm

Eye Pillow
7½" wide x 3½" long/19cm wide x 9cm long

MATERIALS

- 1 skein 1¾oz/50g (each approx 156yds/144m) of Lang/Berroco *La-Se-Ta* (silk②) in #7620 blue, #7673 aqua and #7658 green
- One pair size 3 (3.25mm) needles *or size to obtain gauges*
- 4" x 4"/10cm x 10cm and 4" x 8"/10cm x 21.5cm silk pouch insert filled with lavender
- Tapestry needle

GAUGES

- 28 sts and 36 rows over 4"/10cm in lace pat using size 3 (3.25mm) needles.
- 24 sts and 40 rows over 4"/10cm in St st using size 3 (3.25mm) needles.
Take time to check gauges.

SACHET (make 2 pieces)

FRONT
Cast on 28 sts and work in St st for 3 rows.
Beg lace pat: Row 1 (RS) K2, work first st of chart, work 6-st rep 3 times, work last 6 sts of chart, k2. Cont in pat as established, keeping first and last 2 sts in St st, until piece measures 3¾"/9.5cm from beg, end with a WS row. Work in St st for 3 rows. Bind off.

BACK
Cast on 24 sts and work in St st for 4"/10cm. Bind off.

EYE PILLOW (make 2 pieces)

FRONT
Cast on 52 sts and work in St st for 3 rows.
Beg lace pat: Row 1 (RS) K2, work first st of chart, work 6-st rep 7 times, work last 6 sts of chart, k2. Cont in pat as established, keeping first and last 2 sts in St st, until piece measures 3¼"/8.5cm from beg, end with a WS row. Work in St st for 3 rows. Bind off.

BACK
Cast on 46 sts. Work in St st for 3½"/9 cm. Bind off.

FINISHING
Sew 3 sides tog, leaving 1 side open. Insert pouch. Sew rem side closed.

Stitch key

	k on RS, p on WS
O	yarn over
⊼	k2tog
⅄	ssk
⅄	sk2p

LACE PAT

6-st rep

LINEN AND LACE PILLOWS

Soft pastels lend a graceful note

Linen bed pillows trimmed in matching cotton borders, designed by Mari Lynn Patrick. Based on household linens from the 19th century, the pillows are updated in fresh pastels with snap closures for easy care.

SIZE

14"/35.5cm square

MATERIALS

■ 1 1¾oz/50g ball (each approx 227yd/210m) of Lang/Berroco *Marisa* (cotton ①) in #905 light yellow or, #992 light green or #909 pink

■ One pair size 2 (2.75mm) needles *or size to obtain gauge*

■ ½yd/.5m of 60"/152cm wide coordinating linen

■ 3 large snaps

■ Matching thread

■14" x 14"/35.5cm x 35.5cm pillow form

GAUGE

Yellow and Green edges measure 1¾"/4.5cm wide; Pink edge measures 1½"/4cm wide using size 2 (2.75mm) needles

YELLOW AND GREEN EDGES

Cast on 17 sts.

**Row 1 (RS) *Yo, k1, yo, k2, [k2tog] twice, k2, yo, k2tog, k1*, [yo, k2tog] twice, k1.

Row 2 and all WS rows K3, yo, k2tog, purl to end.

Row 3 *Yo, k3, yo, k1, [k2tog] twice, k1*, yo, k2tog, k1, [yo, k2tog] twice, k1.

Row 5 *Yo, k5, yo, [k2tog] twice*, yo, k2tog, k1, [yo, k2tog] twice, k1.

Row 7 *Yo, k3, k2tog*, k2, [yo, k2tog] twice, k1, [yo, k2tog] twice, k1.

Row 8 Rep row 2. Rep rows 1-8 a total of 17 times—piece measures 14" from beg.

Beg Corner

Short row 1 (over 12 sts). Rep between *'s of row 1, turn.

Short row 2 and all even short rows Sl 1, p to end.

Short row 3 (over 9 sts) Rep between *'s of row 3, turn.

Short row 5 (over 9 sts) Rep between *'s of row 5, turn.

Short row 7 (over 5 sts) Rep between *'s of row 7, turn.

Short row 8 Sl 1, p4.** Rep between **'s 3 times more. Bind off.

FINISHING

Cut two 15"/38cm squares from linen fabric. With RS tog, sew around 3 sides with ½"/1.25cm seam. Turn right side out and press. Press ½"/1.25cm to WS along open edge. Top stitch around all sides and openings ¼"/.6cm from edges. Sew through both thicknesses of open side for 1½"/.6cm in from each corner. Sew three snaps to inside of pillow flaps for closures. Pin lace edge carefully around square, matching corners. Sew cast-on edge to bound-off edge. With thread, whip stitch to very edge of pillow square. After sewing, steam block carefully to soften and loosen up edge.

PINK EDGE

Cast on 10 sts.

Note Yo twice counts as 2 sts, that is, on the foll row, work 2 sts into double yo.

Row 1 K3, [yo, k2tog] twice, yo twice, k2tog, k1.

Row 2 K3, p1, k2, [yo, k2tog] twice, k1.

Row 3 K3, [yo, k2tog] twice, k1, yo twice, k2tog, k1.

Row 4 K3, p1, k3, [yo, k2tog] twice, k1.

Row 5 K3, [yo, k2tog] twice, k2, yo twice, k2tog, k1.

Row 6 K3, p1, k4, [yo, k2tog] twice, k1.

Row 7 K3, [yo, k2tog] twice, k6.

Row 8 Bind off 3 sts, k4, [yo, k2tog] twice, k1. Rep rows 1-8 for pat rep a total of 17 times. Piece measures 14"/35.5cm from beg.

Beg Corner

Short row 1 Rep row 1.

Short row 2 K3, p1, k2, yo, k2tog, turn.

Short row 3 [Yo, k2tog] twice, k1, yo twice, k2tog, k1, turn.

Short row 4 K3, p1, k3, turn.

Short row 5 Yo, k2tog, k2, yo twice, k2tog, k1, turn.

Short row 6 K3, p1, k2, turn.

Short row 7 K6, turn.

Short row 8 Bind off 3 sts, k2, turn.

Short row 9 Yo twice, k2tog, k1. *Beg with row 2, work pat rep 17 times more. Work corner rows 1-9. * Rep between *'s twice more. Bind off.

FINISHING

Work same as for Yellow and Green edges.

NOTES

RESOURCES

US RESOURCES

Write to the yarn companies listed below for purchasing and mail-order information.

BERROCO, INC.
14 Elmdale Road
P.O. Box 367
Uxbridge, MA 01569

BROWN SHEEP CO., INC.
100662 County Road 16
Mitchell, NE 69357

CLASSIC ELITE YARNS, INC.
12 Perkins Street
Lowell, MA 01854
www.classiceliteyarns.com

COATS PATONS
1001 Roselawn Avenue
Toronto, Ontario M6B 1B8

COLINETTE
distributed by
Unique Kolours

DALE OF NORWAY, INC.
N16 W23390 Stoneridge Drive
Suite A
Waukesha, WI 53188

GEDIFRA
distributed by Muench Yarns

JCA/REYNOLDS
35 Scales Lane
Townsend, MA 01469

JO SHARP
distributed by Classic Elite
Yarns, Inc.

LANG
distributed by Berroco, Inc.

LION BRAND YARNS
34 West 15th Street
New York, NY 10011
www.lionbrand.com

MANOS DEL URUGUAY
distributed by
Simpson Southwick

MUENCH YARNS
118 Ricardo Road
Mill Valley, CA 94941-2461

ONE WORLD BUTTON SUPPLY CO.
41 Union Square West
Room 311
New York, NY 10003

PATONS
distributed by Coats Patons

PHILDAR
422 East Vermijo
Colorado Springs, CO 80903

PLYMOUTH YARNS
P.O. Box 28
Bristol, PA 19007

REYNOLDS
distributed by
JCA/Reynolds

ROWAN
distributed by
Westminster Fibers

SIMPSON SOUTHWICK
1-800-843-3484

SKACEL COLLECTION
P.O. Box 88110
Seattle, WA 98138-2110

STACY CHARLES COLLECTION
1059 Manhattan Avenue
Brooklyn, NY 11222

TAHKI IMPORTS LTD.
11 Graphic Place
Moonachie, NJ 07074

UNIQUE KOLOURS
1428 Oak Lane
Downingtown, PA 19335

WESTMINSTER FIBERS
5 Northern Boulevard
Amherst, NH 03031

CANADIAN RESOURCES

Write to US resources for mail-order availability of yarns not listed.

CLASSIC ELITE
distributed by S. R. Kertzer Ltd.

CLECKHEATON
distributed by Diamond Yarns

COATS PATONS
1001 Roselawn Avenue
Toronto, ON M6B 1B8

COLINETTE
distributed by Diamond Yarns

DIAMOND YARNS
9697 St. Laurent
Montreal, PQ H3L 2N1 or
1450 Lodestar Rd. Unit #4
Toronto, ON M3J 3C1

ESTELLE DESIGNS & SALES LTD.
Units 65/67
2220 Midland Avenue
Scarborough, ON M1P 3E6

JO SHARP
distributed by Estelle Designs & Sales Ltd.

S. R. KERTZER LTD.
105A Winges Road
Woodbridge, ON L4L 6C2

LANG
distributed by
R. Stein Yarn Corp.

PATONS
distributed by Coats Patons

PHILDAR
Difference G. Brui Inc.
20 des Cedres
Ile Bizard, PQ H9C 1N9

R. STEIN YARN CORP
5800 St-Denis
Suite 303
Montreal, PQ H2S 3L5

ROWAN
distributed by Diamond Yarns

TAHKI
distributed by Estelle Designs & Sales Ltd.

UK RESOURCES

Not all yarns are available in the UK. For yarns not available, either make a comparable substitute or contact the US manufacturer for purchasing and mail-order information.

COATS CRAFTS UK
distributors of Patons
P.O. Box 22
The Lingfield Estate
Darlington
Co Durham DL1 1YQ
Tel: 01325-365457 .

COLINETTE YARNS LTD.
Units 2-5
Banwy Industrial Estate
Llanfair Caereinion
Powys SY21 OSG
Tel: 01938-810128

KILCARRA YARN LTD.
distributors of *Donegal Tweed*
Kilcar
Co Donegal
Ireland
Tel: 00-353-73-38055

In the UK Cleckheaton is sold as Jarol Super Saver D.K.

JAROL LTD.
White Rose Mills
Cape Street
Canal Road
Bradford, BD1 4RN
Tel: 0274-392274

ROWAN YARNS
Green Lane Mill
Holmfirth
West Yorks HD7 1RW
Tel: 01484-681881

VOGUE KNITTING PILLOWS

Editor-in-Chief
TRISHA MALCOLM

Art Director, Butterick® Company, Inc
JOE VIOR

Book Designer
CHRISTINE LIPERT

Senior Editor
CARLA S. SCOTT

Managing Editor
DARYL BROWER

Associate Knitting Editor
TEVA MARGARET DURHAM

Technical Illustration Editor
LILA P. CHIN

Instructions Coordinator
CHARLOTTE PARRY

Yarn Coordinator
VERONICA MANNO

Instruction Writer
GITTA SCHRADE

Editorial Coordinators
KATHLEEN KELLY
ANNEMARIE McNAMARA

Page Building
DAVID JOINNIDES

Photography
BRIAN KRAUS, NYC
Photographed at Butterick Studios

Project Directors
MARTHA MORAN
CAROLINE POLITI

Publishing Consultant
MIKE SHATZKIN, THE IDEALOGICAL COMPANY

■

President and CEO, Butterick® Company, Inc
JAY H. STEIN

Executive Vice President and Publisher, Butterick® Company, Inc
ART JOINNIDES